D1519971

CAREERS IN THE
US ARMY

Earl Rice Jr.

Enslow Publishing

101 W. 23rd Street
Suite 240
New York, NY 10011
USA

enslow.com

Published in 2016 by Enslow Publishing, LLC.
101 W. 23rd Street, Suite 240, New York, NY 10011

Library of Congress Cataloging-in-Publication Data

Rice, Earle.
 Careers in the US Army / Earle Rice, Jr.
   pages cm. — (Careers in the US Armed Forces)
 Includes bibliographical references and index.
 Summary: "Describes career opportunities in the US Army"—Provided by publisher.
 Audience: Grades 7-8.
 ISBN 978-0-7660-6943-5
 1. United States. Army—Vocational guidance—Juvenile literature. 2. United States. Army—Juvenile literature. I. Title.
 UB323.E47 2015
 355.0023'73—dc23

                    2015015137

Printed in the United States of America

To Our Readers: We have done our best to make sure all Web site addresses in this book were active and appropriate when we went to press. However, the author and the publisher have no control over and assume no liability for the material available on those Web sites or on any Web sites they may link to. Any comments or suggestions can be sent by e-mail to customerservice@enslow.com.

Portions of this book originally appeared in the book *The U.S. Army and Military Careers.*

Photo Credits: AP Images, pp. 99, 106; CENTCOM/Getty Images News/ Getty Images pp. 9, 10; Christine Yarusi (series logo); DoD photo, pp. 63, 109, 110; DoD photo by Lance Cpl. James F. Cline III, U.S. Marine Corps, p. 77; DoD photo by Petty Officer 2nd Class Walter J. Pels, U.S. Navy, p. 4; DoD photo by Staff Sgt. Samuel Bendet, U.S. Air Force, p. 55; DoD photo by Tech. Sgt. John M. Foster, U.S. Air Force, p. 68; Education Images/UIG via Getty Images, p. 71; Eric BOUVET/Gamma-Rapho via Getty Images, p. 57; Larry Burrows/The LIFE Picture Collection/Getty Images, p. 51; Library of Congress, Prints and Photographs Division, pp. 31, 47; MICHEL GANGNE/AFP/Getty Images, p. 56; MPI/Archive Photos/Getty Images, pp. 15, 23, 29; Photo12/UIG via Getty Images, p. 52; Pictorial Parade/Archive Photos/Getty Images, p. 36; Steve Cukrov/Shutterstock.com (chapter openers); Straight 8 Photography/Shutterstock.com, p. 1 (top left); ullstein bild/ullstein bild via Getty Images, p. 20; Universal History Archive/UIG via Getty Images, pp. 18, 34; U.S. Air Force photo/ National Archives and Records Administration/Wikimedia Commons/Pilots of the 332nd Fighter Group.jpg/public domain, p. 72; U.S. Air Force photo by Staff Sgt. Dallas Edwards, p. 7; U.S. Army Center of Military History, p. 41; U.S. Army Corps of Engineers file photo, p. 60; U.S. Army photo, pp. 11, 78, 90, 95, 100, 101, 102; U.S Army photo/173rd Airborne Brigade/Wikimedia Commons/ Milton Lee Olive.jpg/public domain, p. 74; U.S. Army photo by Ashley Cross, p. 86; U.S. Army photos by Cpl. Hwang Joon-hyun, p. 103; U.S. Army photo by Sgt Fay Conroy, p. 96; U.S. Army photo by Sgt. Matthew C. Moeller, p. 64; U.S. Marine Corps photo by Lance Cpl. Patricia D. Lockhart, p. 94; U.S. National Archives and Records Administration/Wikimedia Commons/Warkorea American Soldiers.jpg/public domain, p. 48; U.S. Navy photo by Mass Communication Specialist 2nd Class Gina Wollman, p. 107; U.S. Navy photo by MC1 Bill Steele, 7th Mobile Public Affairs Detachment, p. 84; videodet/iStock/Thinkstock (top right); W. Eugene Smith/The LIFE Picture Collection/Getty Images, p. 43.

Cover Credits: Straight 8 Photography/Shutterstock.com (top left); videodet/iStock/Thinkstock (top right); DoD photo by Petty Officer 1st Class Daniel N. Woods, U.S. Navy (bottom); Christine Yarusi (series logo).

CONTENTS

1   Soldier Stories **5**

2   Evolution of an American Army........... **13**

3   War and Westward Ho! **21**

4   World at War **32**

5   Cold Relations and Hot Wars............. **45**

6   America under Attack
       and Fighting Back......................... **58**

7   Diversity in the Ranks **69**

8   Active and Reserve Forces................. **80**

9   Career Paths for Soldiers **92**

10   Shaping the Army of Tomorrow........... **105**

       Appendix: Salaries in the Army **109**

       Timeline.................................. **111**

       Chapter Notes **114**

       Glossary................................. **121**

       Further Reading **123**

       Index.................................... **125**

US Army soldiers provide security for an Army batallion providing humanitarian aid to Iraqi villagers.

SOLDIER STORIES

Dawn was breaking on the fifth day of Operation Iraqi Freedom. A convoy of soldiers in eighteen trucks and Humvees rumbled out of the night toward the Iraqi market town of Nasiriyah. It was March 23, 2003.

Ambush Alley

Thirty-three soldiers, most of them from 507th Maintenance Company, were struggling to keep up with the rapidly advancing 3rd Infantry Division. They were rushing to help set up Patriot antimissile batteries at Najaf. The rapid run from Kuwait in soft sand had been tough on the trucks. Some had run out of gas; others had gotten stuck in the sand repeatedly. Vehicles at the front of the division were already 130 miles ahead of the 507th. In its dash to Baghdad, the 3rd Infantry could not delay while support units kept pace.

The 507th consisted of personnel trained as supply clerks, cooks, mechanics, computer technicians, and so on. All soldiers carry weapons and are trained to use them. Despite their weapons and training, none of these support soldiers expected to see frontline action. But as so often happens in war, a chance happening intervened in best-laid plans.

Just south of Nasiriyah, the 507th convoy missed a left turn to bypass the city. Instead, it rumbled straight through town. Captain Troy King soon realized the convoy had missed its turnoff. He ordered it back through the city. The line of trucks retraced its route on the main road that would soon become known as Ambush Alley.

Alert to possible danger, Captain King ordered his soldiers to lock and load their weapons. His instructions came none too soon. Suddenly, the convoy came under heavy attack. Fire from AK-47 automatic weapons and rocket-propelled grenades (RPGs) tore into the line of trucks. *AMBUSH!* It was an attack by a party of irregular fighters known as *fedayeen* (martyrs).

Amid the swirling dust and confusion, the fire seemed to come from everywhere. Armed and hostile Iraqis appeared out of every house. "It was a whole city, and we were shot from front, rear, left," recalled Sergeant James Riley. "It was like being in the middle of a parking lot and everyone is shooting at you."[1]

Pickup trucks loaded with fedayeen insurgents in civilian clothes and black masks chased the Americans back through town. The support soldiers fought back, but sand and dirt from caravanning across the desert jammed their weapons. Trucks slammed into one another in the running battle. Several broke down again. Some of the Americans escaped

In Iraq, CH-47 Chinook helicopters escort a convoy of US and Iraqi Army Soldiers back to their base after the completion of their part in a combat operation.

the ambush; others were less fortunate. US authorities reported twelve soldiers missing that day. Among the missing Americans was a nineteen-year-old private first class from West Virginia named Jessica Lynch.

Jessica's Tale

Shortly after the ambush at Nasiriyah, the Arab television network Al Jazeera ran footage of captured American soldiers. The captives looked badly mistreated. Several dead bodies appeared behind them. At US Central Command (CentCom) headquarters in Doha, Qatar, coalition commander General Tommy R. Franks put out an urgent statement to his forces:

Versatile Vehicle

The M988 Humvee is a sturdy, four-by-four-wheeled, tactical vehicle. It can operate in all types of terrain. Its odd name comes from its acronym, HMMWV. It stands for high-mobility multipurpose wheeled vehicle. The Humvee is also called Hummer.

The Humvee is manufactured by AM General. It carries two crew members and six passengers. It entered service in 1985. The Hummer is the US Army's all-purpose vehicle. It replaced the Jeep of World War II fame. The Hummer is large enough to carry several types of weapons systems. These include antitank guided missiles and surface-to-air missiles. The Hummer readily adapts to a variety of missions. Its many uses include weapons carrier, utility vehicle, squad carrier, and ambulance.

"I want to execute a quick, well thought out plan to repatriate surviving US military personnel. The plan will be executed on short order once we have a location."[2]

On March 30, 2003, a US unit near Nasiriyah received a tip from a brave Iraqi. The injured Jessica Lynch had been taken to a local hospital. She had sustained a broken arm, ankle, and foot, and a back injury when an RPG had struck her truck. Lynch had tried to fire back, but her M16 was jammed with grit. In the chaos, she never got it to work.

At Doha, Franks issued an order to the US Special Operations Command: "Put an op[eration] together and get her out of there. Use all the assets you need."[3]

Two days later, on April 1, a "snatch squad" consisting of US Marines, Navy SEALs (sea-air-land commandos), and Army Rangers descended on the hospital in a Blackhawk helicopter in the dead of night. The commandos entered the hospital and quickly located Lynch's room. They approached her bed, calling her name. Lynch lay still with her head under the covers. She was frightened and unaware of what was happening. One of her rescuers said, "Jessica Lynch, we're United States soldiers and we're here to protect you and take you home."[4]

Jessica Lynch slipped the covers down and said, "I'm an American soldier, too."[5]

Indeed, she was. The elite warriors of the Special Forces team strapped Lynch to a stretcher. They swept her off to the waiting helicopter and eventual safety. A later account

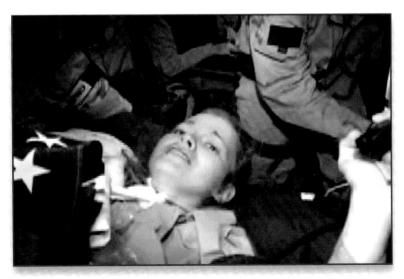

After a special force "snatch squad" rescued Private Jessica Lynch, the 19-year-old was loaded into a military helicopter and shuttled safely out of Iraq.

US soldiers carried Lynch off the helicopter under secrecy in the dead of night. Lynch has moved on to civilian life but still carries the traumatic experience with her.

showed that eleven of her comrades were killed in Ambush Alley or slain in captivity. The men and women of the 507th were American soldiers, too. Their sacrifices honor the US Army's warrior heritage.

Today, back in civilian life, Jessica Lynch is now a mother, teacher, and motivational speaker in her hometown of Charlestown, West Virginia. She is working on a master's degree. She told *Today*'s Savannah Guthrie: "Every day I wake up, I have that 'never give up' attitude. As much as I have the up and down days, it doesn't matter as long as you keep it in your mind that you can do anything, that's what it's all about is perseverance."[6]

A Soldier measures one foot with his boot, and places a flag in front of a grave marker at Arlington National Cemetery.

Warrior's Way

"The Army's mission," declares one of its Web sites, "is to fight and win our Nation's wars by providing prompt, sustained land dominance across the full range of military operations and spectrum of conflict in support of combatant commanders."[7] One way American soldiers accomplish this mission is by adhering to a set of principles they call the Warrior Ethos. The principles are fourfold:

◆ I will always place the mission first.

◆ I will never accept defeat.

◆ I will never quit.

◆ I will never leave a fallen comrade.[8]

Today's American soldiers live by these words. Early in their training, they develop selflessness, resolve, persistence, and loyalty. Such qualities make them better soldiers. These traits also make them better citizens and better human beings. From Lexington, Massachusetts, to Baghdad, Iraq, their selfless acts have reflected the Warrior Ethos. Their stories are many and ongoing. Since 1775, American soldiers have served their nation with honor and distinction.

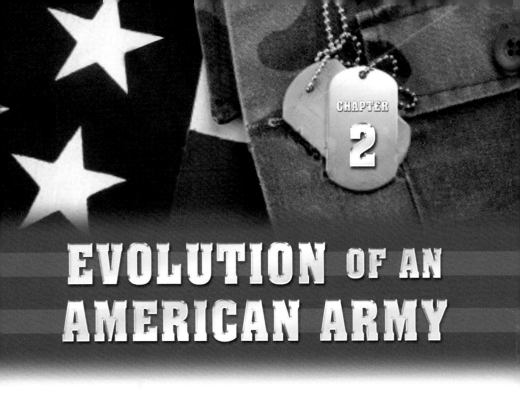

EVOLUTION OF AN AMERICAN ARMY

The US Army has a history as long as the country has been in existence. In 1760, George III ascended the throne of Great Britain and Ireland. The Seven Years' War (1754–63), known in North America as the French and Indian War, was still raging. In its aftermath, the new king found himself facing an enormous war debt. To regain financial solvency, the imperial government instituted a series of taxes in North America. Angry colonists began to raise and drill citizen militias. By the spring of 1775, their anger fueled an open rebellion.

Setting the Standard

On April 14, 1775, Britain ordered General Thomas Gage to seize militia arms stockpiled at Concord, Massachusetts. Gage was the British commander in chief in North America. He was also the governor of the Massachusetts colony. Gage sent seven hundred soldiers to destroy the arms depot.

On their way to Concord, British soldiers met and defeated a small force of Massachusetts militia known as minutemen at Lexington on April 19, 1775. The nickname came from their ability to assemble under arms at a minute's notice. At Concord, the British met a larger force of minutemen. The British were forced to return to Boston. But the shots "heard round the world"[1] had been fired. The American Revolution had begun.

Militia from all over New England laid siege to Boston. The siege would last for almost a year. Meanwhile, the Continental Congress, the main colonial law-making body at the time, adopted the colonial militias as the Continental Army on June 14, 1775. Congress named George Washington to lead the army. The Virginia soldier and planter became the army's first commander in chief.

Washington accepted the command with misgivings. He felt unequal to the huge task at hand. But he soon warmed to the challenge. "The fate of unborn millions will now depend, under God, on the courage and conduct of this army," he told his troops in August 1776. "Our cruel and unrelenting enemy leaves us only the choice of brave resistance or the most abject submission. We have, therefore, to resolve to conquer or die."[2] Under his steady leadership, they conquered. Washington went on to serve two terms as the first American president.

The American Revolution lasted eight years. Congress had favored winning the war by risking all in a single great battle. Washington disagreed. He knew the colonies needed more time to build an army strong enough to defeat the British. In the fall of 1776, Washington changed the risky American strategy of taking a chance on a single large-scale battle to "protract the war."[3] His change of strategy bought

During the Revolutionary War, the Continental Congress named future president George Washington the leader of the Continental Army, the first assemblage of the various colonial militias into one organized unit.

the time he needed to build a strong army. The Continental Army wore down the British over time and America won its independence. After the war ended, the Army disbanded.

Today's US Army has its roots in the Continental Army. It consisted largely of long-term volunteers. Its size ranged roughly from five thousand to twenty thousand soldiers.[4] Soldiers sometimes supplied their own uniforms. Most wore work or hunting clothes. Washington wore the blue and buff of the Virginia militia. Green and brown became the main uniform colors because of locally available dyes. Blue became the official color in 1779.

Regulars of the Continental Army were generally reliable and surprisingly well trained. Foot soldiers used smoothbore muskets with bayonets and American long rifles. Many carried hatchets adopted from the Indians. Cavalry was almost never used. Cannons ranging from 3- to 24-pounders and 5.5- and 8-inch howitzers supported the infantry. A few 18-, 24-, and 32-pounder siege guns were also available.

The Continental Army fought British and Hessian regulars in European-style combat. This orderly style of fighting differed greatly from the unruly style of colonial militias. In practice, tactics evolved. They grew into a blend of British linear formations and frontier-style fighting from concealed positions.

The Continental Army set the standard for its successor in the 1790s. Similarly, George Washington became the model for future US military officers.

To Police and Defend

Congress created the Army of the Constitution in 1789. Congress established it to meet the young nation's needs of frontier policing and defense. It grew out of the first permanent US Army formed in 1784 under the Articles of Confederation. The Articles formed the first national constitution of the independent United States. This tiny force of regulars and militia numbered about eight hundred officers and men. Its size rose and fell as needed to meet and resolve crises.

Also in 1794, President Washington sent General "Mad Anthony" Wayne to put down an Indian uprising near the modern city of Toledo, Ohio. Wayne defeated the Indians in the Battle of Fallen Timbers. The battle lasted less than an hour. It began with a cavalry attack and ended with a bayonet charge. The American Indians, as they said later, "could not stand up against the sharp ends of the guns."[5] In 1795, the ensuing Treaty of Greenville ceded Indian lands to the United States. The treaty ended British influence in the region.

In 1797, John Adams succeeded George Washington as president. Washington returned to Virginia. He died from a throat infection on December 13, 1799. In 1801, Thomas Jefferson became the third US president. He fixed the size of the peacetime army at two regiments of infantry, one of artillery, plus a small corps of engineers. The Army's total strength stood at 3,287.[6]

On March 1, 1802, Congress authorized Jefferson to establish the US Military Academy at West Point, New York. Its primary mission was to train engineering officers for the Army. It opened on July 4, 1802.

Another War With Britain

In 1812, the United States went to war with Great Britain again. The war grew out of harsh British naval practices in Britain's war with France. Britain repeatedly violated the marine rights of neutral nations. American efforts to annex Canada did little to calm the waters of mutual discontent.

The War of 1812 brought great changes to the Army. Its authorized strength grew to almost sixty-three thousand.[7] Actually, enlistments fell far short of authorized numbers. But the Army's performance improved greatly as battle-seasoned officers rose to middle and high ranks. Notable among the new senior officer corps was Winfield Scott. He would later become the commanding general of the Army.

After the war, the Army's chief mission was to prepare for war with a major European power.

Under Presidents James Madison and James Monroe, the Army established permanent general staff bureaus and uniform rules and regulations. These changes helped to improve its management and operations. The Army also built a system of coastal forts. At the same time, Captain Sylvanus Thayer brought new life to the US Military Academy. The school had originally suffered under poor administration. Thayer first championed a strict code of discipline and then instituted a four-year curriculum stressing engineering and mathematics.

Indian Resistance and Relocation

In 1821, Congress again reduced the size of the Army. It now consisted of eleven line regiments. They were supported by several general staff bureaus. The bureaus consisted of quartermaster, engineers, ordnance, medical, and subsistence.

George Washington moved his headquarters to the strategic location of West Point, New York, in 1779. The US Military Academy was established on the site in 1802.

These all reported to the commanding general of the Army. For the next two decades, the Army assisted the government in nation building. It helped to develop and expand the new nation. The Army also played a key role in American Indian management and relocation.

Brigadier General Winfield Scott continued his rise to prominence in the 1830s. Scott commanded US forces in the Black Hawk War in 1832. He also took part in the war against the Seminole Indians in 1836. Two years later, he directed the removal of the Cherokee from South Carolina, Georgia, and Tennessee. On July 5, 1841, Major General Winfield Scott was named commanding general of the Army.

Battles Below the Border

In 1845, the United States annexed Texas. The country now embraced the concept of "Manifest Destiny." The concept referred to the American "right . . . to spread over this whole continent."[8] In 1846, war broke out with Mexico over disputed territorial claims in Texas. At first, Winfield Scott supported General Zachary Taylor's campaigns in Texas and northern Mexico. (A campaign is a long military action.) But Scott changed his mind. He felt that a direct assault on Mexico City was needed to bring a quick end to the war. Scott took personal charge of the campaign in southern Mexico.

Scott led an American invasion force in an unopposed landing at Vera Cruz on March 9, 1847. Under his leadership, the Army then began the long march on Mexico City. Many officers of future fame served under him. They included Ulysses S. Grant, Robert E. Lee, and a number of others.

The Americans fought several key battles against the forces of General Antonio López de Santa Anna of Mexico.

General Winfield Scott led troops to take Vera Cruz before marching them to Mexico City.

They battled at Jalapa, Cerro Gordo, Contreras, Churubusco, Chapultepec, and Mexico City. Under Scott, the Americans won every single battle. Captain "Sam" Grant assessed Scott's performance this way: "Credit is due to the troops engaged, it is true, but the plans and strategies were the general's."[9]

The US-Mexican War ended with the signing of the Treaty of Guadalupe Hidalgo on February 2, 1848. Terms of the treaty ceded about 50 percent of Mexico's land to the United States. The land included the future states of California, Nevada, Arizona, New Mexico, and Utah. Largely through the Army's efficiency, the United States became a continental power. America's boundaries now stretched from the Atlantic to the Pacific. In addition, the conflict with Mexico had served the Army as a training ground for a much larger war still to come.

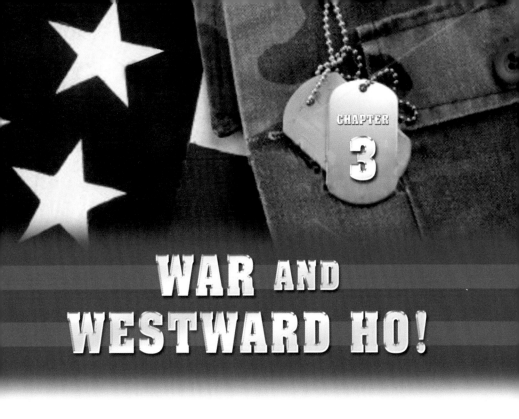

WAR AND WESTWARD HO!

When silence settled over the battlefields of the Mexican-American War, a cry of *Westward Ho!* rang out across the young land. Blue-coated soldiers led the way and provided protection for intrepid adventurers, across prairies and plains, mountains and vales, and on to the shores of the great blue Pacific.

In the 1850s, the Army fought twenty-two distinct wars with American Indians. To meet these new duties, the Army grew to about sixteen to seventeen thousand men.[1] Most of the troops were spread across a million square miles west of the Mississippi.

In 1861, a civil war broke out in the young nation. Northerners and Southerners disagreed on the issues of states' rights, trade and tariffs, and slavery. In 1860, the election of Abraham Lincoln as president had inflamed these issues. Lincoln opposed slavery. Soon after his election, seven (later eleven) Southern states left the Union. They formed the Confederate States of America under President Jefferson Davis.

On April 12, 1861, the Confederates fired on and later seized Fort Sumter, South Carolina. The rebel cannon fire touched off the American Civil War. President Lincoln countered swiftly. A month earlier, he had pledged to "hold, occupy and possess"[2] all federal property and places within Confederate territory. He intended to keep this pledge and he gave the Army the task of preserving the Union.

North vs. South

The Union Army numbered just over sixteen thousand men in April 1861. The Confederacy started the war with an army of about thirty-five thousand men. President Lincoln quickly responded to the attack on Fort Sumter. He called for seventy-five thousand volunteers to put down the Southern revolt.[3] One hundred thousand men answered his call.[4] "So large an army as the government has now on foot, was never before known,"[5] Lincoln exclaimed.

In three months, the Union Army grew to about two hundred thirty-five thousand men.[6] By war's end, the blue-clad Union Army would field almost a million men. Three quarters of a million men in Confederate gray would oppose them. For the first time, the Army was forced to face a crisis of loyalty. Roughly one quarter of its officer corps resigned to support the Confederacy. Both sides necessarily resorted to a draft to maintain troop levels. The more heavily populated North enjoyed a larger base to call on.

In July 1861, Union forces drove toward the Confederate capital of Richmond, Virginia. But before they arrived,

The 96th Pennsylvanian Regiment of the Union Army carries out a drill at Camp Northumberland outside Washington, D.C., during the US Civil War.

Confederate troops defeated them at Bull Run Creek. The South claimed the first victory of the Civil War. Union soldiers retreated back toward Washington, D.C.

Northern forces under General Ulysses S. Grant began the first major campaign in the western theater in 1862. Grant's victories at Fort Donelson in Tennessee gave Northerners heart. Grant called for "an unconditional and immediate surrender."[7] His harsh terms earned him the nickname "Unconditional Surrender," a play on his first two initials. Grant followed his Donelson successes with a stunning victory at Shiloh, Tennessee.

In the East, General Robert E. Lee and his Army of Northern Virginia won several victories in the Seven Days' Battle near Richmond. He then lost at Antietam Creek, near Sharpsburg, Maryland. Lee bounced back to defeat General Ambrose Burnside's Union Army of the Potomac at Fredericksburg, Virginia, in December 1862. Lee scored another shocking victory at Chancellorsville, Virginia, in May of 1863. But the fortunes of war turned in the North's favor two months later.

There a Stone Wall Stands

In July 1861, thirty thousand Union troops under General Irvin McDowell moved toward the Confederate capital of Richmond, Virginia. A strong Confederate force under Generals Pierre Beauregard and Joseph E. Johnston halted McDowell's advance in the First Battle of Bull Run. McDowell tried to turn his enemy's west flank. But General Thomas J. Jackson's Virginia brigade held firm. General Bernard Bee rallied his own Virginia brigade. He shouted, "Look at Jackson's brigade; it stands like a stone wall!"[8] The Southerners forced the Federals to pull back. Both Jackson and his brigade kept the name "Stonewall" for the rest of the war.

On July 4, 1863, Grant opened up the Mississippi to Union forces with a victory at Vicksburg. On the same day, General George Meade's Army of the Potomac defeated General Lee's Virginians at Gettysburg, Pennsylvania. The twin Union triumphs marked the beginning of the end for the Confederacy.

Grant turned in another victory at Chattanooga in September 1863. President Lincoln promoted him to lieutenant general. The president summoned Grant to Washington as general in chief of all the Union forces. The president told Grant to devise a strategy to end the war. Grant started to slowly destroy his Southern foes.

Grant suffered heavy losses in the battles of the Wilderness and Spotsylvania in Virginia. But he began to surround Lee's forces in Petersburg. Grant captured Richmond on April 3, 1865. Lee surrendered to Grant at Appomattox Court House on April 9. Meanwhile, General William T. Sherman's Union forces had marched through Georgia. General Joseph E. Johnston's surrendered to him at Durham Station, North Carolina, on April 26.

The war ended. It had cost about six hundred twenty thousand lives. Battle tactics had not adjusted to the killing capacity of improved weaponry. Outdated formations quickly fell before rapid-firing rifles and cannon. But President Lincoln and the Union Army had saved the Union and rid the nation of slavery.

Rebuilding a Nation

After the Civil War, Congress reduced the one-million-man Union Army to a US Army of twenty-nine thousand by 1871.[9] The Army took on new duties as occupation forces

Guns, Bayonets, and Horses

Advances in technology produced better weaponry for use in the Civil War. Both sides used the rifle musket as the basic infantry weapon. It fired a Minié ball, a tapered, lead projectile. Steel bayonets came in two types—socket and sword. The socket bayonet fit around the front of the muzzle of the rifle. It measured fourteen to eighteen inches long. The sword bayonet had a handle and was shaped like its name suggests. It attached to the side of the barrel of the rifle and extended two feet beyond the muzzle.

Cavalry came into its own during the Civil War. Horse soldiers were armed with sabers, carbines (short rifles), and pistols. The cavalry's most valuable—and expensive—resource was the horse. Cavalrymen usually supplied their own horses. The government replaced those lost in action. In one action-filled month, the Union army provided its cavalry corps with seven thousand horses.[10]

The most common big gun on both sides was the M1857 Napoleon. It fired a 12-pound ball from a smoothbore 1,200-pound bronze tube at ranges from 600 to 1,200 yards. A second gun in wide use was the 10-pound, 2.9-inch bore Parrott gun. Howitzers, 12-, 24-, and 32-inch, were also available.

in the South. It was also used to suppress strife in industrial areas. The Army was the only federal agency with enough men to carry out the many rebuilding tasks in the South.

The Army's primary role during the Reconstruction era was peacekeeping. Its many other duties included such civil matters as regulating commercial law, civil court proceedings, and public education. It also registered voters, held elections, and approved new state constitutions. Rebuilding bridges, operating banks and railroads, and dealing with crooked politicians and petty criminals also kept the Army busy.

One of the Army's most important functions during Reconstruction was to protect the rights of newly freed African Americans. But true freedom would continue to elude African Americans for years to come. "Although the freed man is no longer considered the property of the individual master," wrote German-American politician and journalist Carl Schurtz, "he *is* considered the slave of society."[11]

An Unstoppable Tide

In the late 1860s, the government abandoned its earlier policy of treating much of the West as a vast American Indian reserve. Instead, it gradually introduced a policy of confining American Indians on small tribal reservations. American Indians could either consent to confinement or fight.

Some tribes, such as the Crow of Montana and the Pueblo of the Southwest, agreed to life on the reservation. Others chose to fight. The latter included the western Sioux, Cheyenne, Arapaho, Kiowa, and Comanche on the Great Plains. They were joined by the Bannock and Nez Percé in the northern Rockies. The Apache spread terror across the southwest. The government charged the Army with the task of rounding up and confining the warring tribes. In the wake of the Civil War, the final war to win the West commenced. The battles continued through the 1870s and 1880s.

The American Indians won a few battles, but they did not win a single campaign. Their most notable victory came at the Battle of the Little Bighorn in 1876. Some two thousand Sioux and Cheyenne, led by Chiefs Crazy Horse and Sitting Bull, annihilated an entire battalion of Colonel George Armstrong Custer's 7th Cavalry Regiment in less than an hour.[12] But the victors did not rejoice in their triumph. "There was no dancing nor celebrating of any kind," Wooden Leg, a Cheyenne, recalled later. "Too many people were in mourning."[13]

The clash between the Army and American Indians from 1865 to 1890 became known as the Indian Wars. They raged over the plains, mountains, and deserts of the American West. The fighting was guerrilla-style. It was characterized by skirmishes, pursuits, raids, massacres, expeditions, battles, and campaigns. Each varied in size and intensity. As one soldier complained during a campaign, "the front is all around, and the rear is nowhere."[14]

Blue-coated soldiers included two infantry and two cavalry regiments of African-American troops. The American Indians called them buffalo soldiers. They saw a similarity between the curly hair and dark skin of the soldier and the buffalo. The Army also used a few American Indian scouts. But white soldiers filled most of the enlisted ranks. Many were recent arrivals from Europe.

Basic Army weaponry consisted of single-shot Springfield and seven-shot Spencer rifles, Springfield carbines, Colt .45-caliber revolvers, sabers, Gatling guns, and 12-pound

US Army troops under General George Armstrong Custer were slaughtered at the Battle of the Little Bighorn. The Indian Wars pitted the US Army against American Indians for control of western lands.

howitzers. The Gatling gun was a ten-barrel, crank-revolved weapon capable of firing four hundred rounds a minute. Howitzers could lob two shells a minute. They were not known for accuracy, but they made a lot of noise and raised plenty of dirt. On occasion, they even helped to drive off superior numbers of American Indians.

The Plains Indians were formidable foes. They fought a fast-moving war. American Indian cavalry covered ground at amazing speeds. But they fought in vain against the unstoppable tide of America's westward expansion. The Indian Wars ended in South Dakota at a place called Wounded Knee on December 29, 1890. Thirty-one soldiers and about two hundred Lakota Sioux died in that final battle.

War with Spain

The US Army closed out the nineteenth century with the Spanish-American War in 1898. Trouble erupted when Cuba began its War of Independence against Spain in 1895. American leaders felt that Spain threatened US security. President William McKinley sent the battleship USS *Maine* to protect American interests in Cuba.

On February 15, 1898, the *Maine* exploded for unexplained reasons in Havana harbor. Without proof, the United States blamed Spain for the *Maine*'s explosion. Congress demanded Spain's immediate withdrawal from Cuba. Spain replied by declaring war on the United States. In April, Americans went to war under the stirring battle cry of "Remember the *Maine*!"

The Army ballooned from its peacetime strength of twenty-five thousand to a force of some threehundred thousand.[15] President McKinley ordered actions against the Spanish colonies of Cuba, Puerto Rico, and the Philippine Islands. American ground and naval forces defeated the Spaniards on every front. American soldiers marched into Manila in the Philippines, in August 1898. It was the last offensive action of the war.

War and Westward Ho!

The US Army had diminished in numbers after the Civil War. When war erupted with Spain, volunteer regiments were assembled. Here, Col. Theodore Roosevelt (center) poses with his Rough Riders Volunteer Cavalry in Cuba.

In the Treaty of Paris of 1898, Spain gave up all claim to Cuba. It also ceded Guam, Puerto Rico, and the Philippines to the United States. American soldiers spent the next four years fighting a revolt in the Philippines. The Philippines eventually gained full independence on July 4, 1946.

The war with Spain propelled the United States into the twentieth century as an emerging world power. It would soon be called upon to project its new power in Europe.

WORLD AT WAR

The twentieth century ushered in the age of modern warfare. It began in Europe. The Guns of August opened fire to announce the start of World War I in 1914. Improved artillery and newly developed machine guns ruled the killing fields of a "War to End All Wars." Tanks clambered across trench-lined battlefields fouled by poison gases. Airplanes dueled to the death in the air. And submarine predators sent unwary ships to the bottom of the sea.

Europe's nations split into two armed alliances. They were known as the Triple Entente and the Central Powers. Great Britain, France, and Russia comprised the principal Entente nations. They were commonly called the Allies. The Central Powers consisted chiefly of Germany and Austria-Hungary. Britain and France checked an initial German advance into

France in the First Battle of the Marne in September 1914. The war of movement settled into a static trench war for the next two-and-a-half years.

Addressing Congress on August 19, 1914, US president Woodrow Wilson said, "The United States must be neutral in fact as well as in name."[1] But Germany announced unrestricted submarine warfare in January 1917 and sank the ship, *Lusitania*, with Americans on board. Wilson changed his mind. On April 2, 1917, he told Congress that Germany's new policy threatened US ships. "The world must be made safe for democracy,"[2] he said. The United States declared war on Germany four days later.

By 1916, the conflict in Europe had prompted the United States to prepare for war. Congress allotted funds for defense. The Army bought modern rifles (the Springfield Model 1903), artillery, and field telephones. It began experimenting with machine guns, aircraft, and motor transport. Structurally, it created the nation's first peacetime divisions. These were self-contained-and-supporting fighting units of about ten thousand men.

The Army also explored ways of rapidly expanding its ranks—both regular and National Guard—with well-trained personnel. (The National Guard had grown out of state militias in the decade after the Civil War.) It laid the foundation for the Reserve Officer Training Corps (ROTC). Despite these efforts, the Army remained unprepared for World War I.

President Wilson called for a draft. The Selective Service draft ballooned the peacetime army. It grew from about one hundred thousand regulars to a wartime army of almost 4 million men in eighteen months.[3] General John J. Pershing was named to head the American Expeditionary Force

US General John J. Pershing arrives in France to join the Allies in World War I.

(AEF) that was to fight in Europe. The AEF sailed for France on June 14, 1917.

Tipping the Balance of Power

American soldiers saw limited action in 1917. British and French leaders wanted to merge the Americans into their own divisions. General Pershing fought to keep his AEF together. He wanted the AEF to fight as an American army. Pershing usually got his way and he did this time as well.

In December 1917, an internal revolution forced Russia to make a separate peace with Germany. The armistice with Russia freed German troops for use in the West. In 1918, Germany launched a series of five offensives. They began in March and ended unsuccessfully in mid-July.

Americans joined the battle in May. It soon became obvious that they were not battle ready. Soldiers of the world's leading industrial nation went to war using many British and French weapons. But the Americans overcame shortcomings in arms and equipment. They impressed their veteran German foes with their fighting ability and raw courage.

Germany's fifth offensive ended in the Second Battle of the Marne on July 17, 1918. As in 1914, the tide of battle turned at the Marne River. The next day, the Allies launched a series of counteroffensives. Steady Allied advances recovered most of France and Belgium by October. British, Belgian, French, and American victories across a broad front led to the armistice on November 11, 1918.

In a message to his troops, General Pershing said: "Our Armies, hurriedly raised and hastily trained, met a veteran enemy, and by courage, discipline and skill always defeated

Tennessee Sharpshooter

The most famous rifleman hero of World War I was Alvin C. York. He was a draftee from the backwoods hamlet of Pall Mall, Tennessee.

On October 8, 1918, a large group of Germans surrendered to advancing American soldiers in the Argonne Forest. Moments later, German gunners opened fire on the Americans from hidden machine-gun nests. Their deadly fire killed or wounded half of the Americans. Private First Class York kneeled down and returned fire with his Springfield rifle. He was an expert shot. His keen shooting killed some twenty Germans. He silenced about thirty-five guns.

Alvin C. York

When the firing had stopped, York rounded up 132 remaining Germans with his .45 Colt. He then led his comrades to safety and his prisoners to captivity. For his exceptional heroism, York earned the Medal of Honor. He was promoted to sergeant.

him. . . . Your deeds will live forever on the most glorious pages of America's history."[4]

Pershing's First and Second Armies played key roles in the final Allied offensive in the Meuse-Argonne. Six other American divisions spearheaded Allied offensives elsewhere. The AEF's fresh initiative and added numbers tipped the balance of power.

In concert, the Allies won the war. Arguably, however, they lost the peace.

Harsh Terms

The Treaty of Versailles of 1919 formally concluded World War I. It forced Germany to accept the blame for Allied losses and to pay major reparations. The treaty further reduced and restricted the size of Germany's land and military. These harsh terms were intended to prevent Germany from ever becoming strong enough to wage another war. But they also produced an economic depression and a bitterness among the German people.

In the 1920s, German dictator Adolf Hitler rose to power by eroding the penalties of the Versailles treaty. Of the treaty, Hitler wrote: "In the boundlessness of its oppression, the shamelessness of its demands, lies the greatest propaganda weapon for the reawakening of a nation's dormant spirits of life."[5]

Interim Innovations

After the war, the US Army cut back rapidly. It returned to an all-volunteer, peacetime army of about two hundred twenty-four thousand men.[6] Congress authorized a voluntary training program for an expanded National Guard and organized reserve. But it kept tight control on other military funding. The Army soon lacked funds for creating a modern armored force. By the mid-1930s, it could not field a single combat-ready division.

War clouds began gathering over Europe in 1935. Congress gradually increased the Army's size. A year later, the Army adopted the .30-caliber Garand (M1) semiautomatic rifle to replace the 1903 Springfield. During the 1930s, it perfected the mobile 105-mm howitzer. It would become the Army's chief big gun of World War II.

The Army also developed light and medium tanks. It acquired new vehicles of various kinds. Horsepower yielded to motor power. Cavalrymen rode mounts of steel. The Army reduced the size of an infantry division to three regiments instead of four. The smaller division quickened the mobility of a mechanized army.

Arsenal of Democracy

On September 1, 1939, Germany's Wehrmacht (armed forces) invaded Poland. World War II began in Europe. At first, Americans wanted no part of another war in Europe. But Germany's defeat of France in June 1940 sounded an alarm across the sea. Britain stood alone between America and Hitler's new European fortress.

Fears of US involvement in Europe's war prompted Congress to further expand US regular forces. Congress planned to create a better-armed field force of 1.5 million by mid-1941. It also federalized the National Guard, called up the reserves, and initiated the nation's first peacetime draft.

In December 1940, President Franklin D. Roosevelt told the nation, "There is no demand for sending an American

Expeditionary Force outside our own borders."[7] He added, "We must be the great arsenal of democracy."[8]

In March 1941, Congress authorized a Lend-Lease program to send war matériel to Britain. In return, Britain allowed the United States to set up military bases on British territories in the Western Hemisphere.

In June 1941, Hitler invaded the Soviet Union. The United States expanded its Lend-Lease program to include the Soviets. The Lend-Lease program was clearly not the act of a neutral nation. America moved closer to war. It came in a most unexpected way.

Date of Infamy

World War II struck the United States on Sunday morning, December 7, 1941. Japanese aircraft attacked US military installations in Hawaii and the Philippines. President Roosevelt called it "a date which will live in infamy."[9] America declared war on Japan. Germany declared war on the United States. American soldiers, called GIs (from the words "government issue"), went to war against the Axis nations of Germany, Italy, and Japan.

Great Britain and the United States became allies again. They agreed on a "Germany first" strategy. They planned to fight a holding action against Japan in the Pacific until victory was won in Europe. Japanese advances in the Pacific required more Allied attention than first anticipated. But the Allied strategy stayed mostly on track.

The US Army of mostly draftees established itself as a powerful and flexible war machine in World War II. The Army numbered more than 8 million officers and men. It fielded ninety-eight combat divisions. A large tactical and strategic air force supported it. The Army further maintained many other service organizations needed to wage a global war. American soldiers again fought bravely and effectively in a variety of environments.

Under General Dwight D. Eisenhower's leadership, the US Army began its campaign against Germany in November 1942. Allied armies drove Field Marshal Erwin Rommel's Armeegruppe Afrika (Army Group Africa) out of North Africa. Untested GIs matured in battle. Allied armies swept across Sicily and through Italy in 1943 and 1944. Italy was defeated by 1944.

On June 6, 1944, the Allies landed in Normandy, France. They started down the long road to Berlin. At the same time, Soviet forces advanced toward Germany from the East. Eleven months later, the German government surrendered unconditionally to the Allies on May 8, 1945. World War II in Europe had ended.

Field Marshal Erwin Rommel commanded two German armies in Normandy. Of the Americans, he said: "Starting from scratch an army has been created in the very minimum of time, which, in equipment, armament and organization of arms, surpasses anything the world has yet seen."[10] The Allies now focused their attention on Japan.

Beginning at Guadalcanal in August 1942, the United States had launched a two-pronged attack against Japanese forces in the Southwest and Central Pacific. General Douglas MacArthur commanded US Army and Allied operations in New Guinea and the Philippines. Admiral Chester W. Nimitz directed US naval forces in an island-hopping campaign across the Central Pacific. The twin offensives converged at the Japanese-held island of Okinawa. US forces defeated

On June 6, 1944, otherwise known as D-Day, US troops arrived on the beaches of France. Made up mostly of draftees, the US Army grew in size and strength during World War II.

Most Decorated Soldier

Audie Leon Murphy was the most decorated American soldier of World War II. Murphy was born near Farmersville, Texas, in 1924. He enlisted in the Army in 1942. Corporal Murphy fought across North Africa and up the Italian peninsula with the US 3rd Infantry Division (ID). After battling at Anzio, the 3rd ID landed on the beaches of southern France in August 1944.

In his first action in France, Murphy earned the Distinguished Service Cross. He wiped out a German machine-gun nest. Murphy next picked up a Purple Heart near Besançon in September. On October 2 and 5, he earned Silver Stars. A week later, he received a battlefield commission to second lieutenant. In late October, a sniper's bullet put him in the hospital for two months. The hip wound he sustained earned him another Purple Heart.

Returning to action in January 1945, Murphy assumed command of the 3rd ID's Company B, 1st Battalion, 15th Infantry Regiment. Near Colmar, he single-handedly turned back a German infantry company and six Mark VI Tiger tanks. Murphy ordered his company to withdraw. He stayed behind to cover their retreat. Murphy jumped on a burning US tank destroyer. He opened fire on the advancing Germans with a .50-caliber machine gun. Fifty Germans died. The attack stopped. Murphy received the Medal of Honor for his heroism. In all, he earned thirty-seven medals and decorations.

After the war, Murphy enjoyed a long, successful career as a movie actor. He died in a plane crash at the age of 46. Because of his distinguished military service, Murphy was interred in Arlington National Cemetery.

Army soldiers participated in the Pacific Theater under General MacArthur. Here, a soldier mans a machine gun as the Allies attempt to take Okinawa.

a stubborn enemy in the last battle of World War II. The fighting officially ended on July 2, 1945.

On August 6, 1945, a US B-29 bomber dropped the first ever atomic bomb, called Little Boy, on the Japanese city of Hiroshima. Three days later, another B-29 dropped another atomic bomb, called Fat Man, on Nagasaki. The bombs leveled both cities. The Atomic Age had begun. On August 11, the Soviets entered the war against Japan. Japanese leaders formally surrendered to the Allies on September 2, 1945.

After World War II, the Army again plunged into a massive demobilization mode. As world events would soon show, its cutback of forces came too soon and cut too deep.

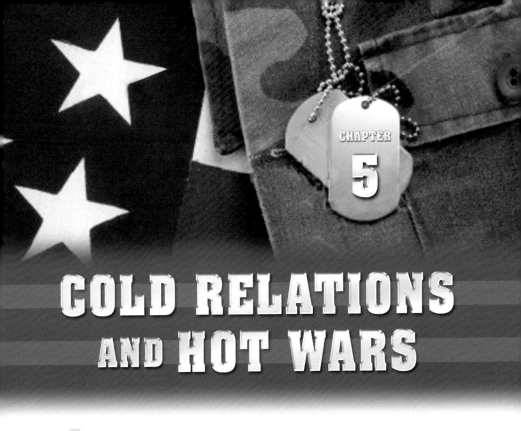

COLD RELATIONS AND HOT WARS

At the end of World War II, the Allied Powers—the United States, the Soviet Union, Great Britain, France, and China—founded the United Nations (UN) in 1945. It was formed In San Francisco to maintain world peace and security, a noble purpose not easily achieved.

Soon after World War II, the United States and the Soviet Union began an intense rivalry. The United States grew more and more concerned about Soviet domination in Eastern Europe. Relations between the two nations turned cold. This period of frigid—often hostile—relations between East and West became known as the Cold War. It would last for almost a half century.

In 1949, twelve Western powers formed a military alliance. Their aim was to defend Western Europe against Soviet expansion. It was called the North Atlantic Treaty

Organization (NATO). Its chief members were the United Kingdom, France, Canada, and the United States. One provision of NATO's charter stated that "an armed attack against one or more of them . . . shall be considered an attack against them all."[1] It was meant to discourage Soviet aggression.

The United States was now committed to defending Western Europe. Still, the Army cut back from 8 million men and ninety-eight divisions in 1945 to five hundred ninety thousand men and ten divisions in 1950.[2] In 1949, the Soviets tested an atomic bomb. As a result, the Army added four divisions to the two divisions already in Europe.

Intervention

On June 25, 1950, the US Army went to war again—not in Europe but in Asia. At the end of World War II, the United States and the Soviet Union occupied Korea. They divided Korea into two temporary zones at the 38th parallel. Later attempts to reunify the divided country failed. The Koreans adopted a Communist government in the north and a democratic government in the south. War erupted when North Korean President Kim Il Sung attempted to reunite Korea by force. The UN and the United States intervened on behalf of South Korea.

US president Harry Truman named General Douglas MacArthur supreme commander of UN forces in the Far East. American troops began landing in South Korea from Japan on July 1. "There was now no doubt!" Truman wrote later. "The Republic of Korea needed help at once if it was not to be overrun."[3]

The North Korean armies quickly drove the UN forces to the southern tip of the Korean peninsula. On July 29, US

Infantry soldiers shield themselves from exploding mortar shells, near the Hantan River in central Korea. The Army joined the UN forces sent to Korea to support the south against Kim Il Sung's Communist government.

Eighth Army commander General Walton H. Walker issued a "stand or die" order to his faltering 25th Division. It said: "If some of us must die, we will die fighting together. . . . I want everybody to understand that we are going to hold this line."[4] UN forces held at the Pusan Perimeter.

General MacArthur then carried out a seaborne landing at Inchon with Army and Marine forces. His daring action cut off the North Korean invaders. He then chased their fleeing armies northward to the Chinese border. Unexpectedly,

An entrenched machine-gun crew strategizes against the North Korean advance during the Korean War. UN forces were not entirely successful in their attempts to stop Communist North Korea.

China entered the war and drove the UN forces back below the 38th parallel.

Not unlike World War I, the Korean War settled into trench warfare. UN forces fought along a main line of resistance and on outposts in front of the lines. They fought with mostly outmoded weapons from World War II. In the skies, however, new P-80 Shooting Stars and MiG-17 jets entered combat for the first time. The two sides agreed to a cease-fire in July 1953. A formal end to the war has never been reached.

Medal for Mitchell

On the night of November 5, 1950, Companies E and G of the US 19th Infantry Regiment occupied Hill 123, four miles north of the Chongchon River. Corporal Mitchell Red Cloud, a Winnebago American Indian, manned a critical listening post. Toward morning, he sensed movement in the brushy hillside below him. Then—suddenly—a line of Chinese soldiers emerged from the brush. Red Cloud shouted a warning to his men. He opened fire on the intruders with his Browning automatic rifle (BAR).

Six enemy soldiers went down. More kept coming. Red Cloud kept firing his BAR, burst after heavy burst. More Chinese fell. Still more came on. Other members of his platoon soon joined the battle. M1 rifles cracked. Machine guns chattered. The br-r-r-urp br-r-r-urp of Chinese "burp" guns answered back. Chinese soldiers swarmed forward. Red Cloud kept firing until a burst from a burp gun silenced him.

Just as the Chinese appeared ready to overrun the American positions, the deep hammering of Red Cloud's BAR started up again. The mortally wounded corporal had regained consciousness. He struggled out of his foxhole. With one arm wrapped around a small tree for support, he resumed pumping BAR fire into the enemy. Five minutes later, enemy attackers silenced him forever. But Red Cloud's last stand had given his comrades time to regroup and hold the hill. They later found more than twenty dead Chinese in front of his foxhole. Mitchell Red Cloud was awarded the Medal of Honor posthumously.

Valor without Victory

President Dwight D. Eisenhower adopted a new defense policy. It emphasized nuclear deterrence. The Army assumed a secondary role of putting out global "brushfires." Presidents John F. Kennedy and Lyndon B. Johnson moved away from a nuclear policy. They restored the Army as the nation's first line of conventional defense in Europe. They further called on the Army to combat Communist insurgencies in Third World countries. Vietnam became the focus of this policy.

In 1954, the Communist forces of Ho Chi Minh defeated the French in the First Indochina War. Vietnam was divided, pending free elections in 1956. But Ho Chi Minh decided to reunite the country by force. Vietcong fighters started a guerrilla war in South Vietnam in 1959.

In 1961, President Kennedy vowed that America would "pay any price" to help its friends stop the spread of communism.[5] Premier Nikita Khrushchev of the Soviet Union answered Kennedy. He promised to support "wars of national liberation."[6]

Kennedy sent more than fifteen thousand military personnel to help South Vietnam.[7] They included Green Beret Special Forces and advisers. After Kennedy's assassination in November 1963, President Lyndon Johnson continued sending support troops to South Vietnam.

Early in August 1964, North Vietnamese patrol boats attacked US destroyers in the Tonkin Gulf. President Johnson asked Congress for a resolution empowering him to "take all necessary measures to repel an armed attack against the forces of the United States and to prevent further aggression."[8]

The Army was enlisted to stop the threat of communism in Vietnam. The war ended up draining the Army's resources.

US Army soldiers embark on a reconnaissance mission in Vietnam during the war.

On August 7, the Senate approved the Tonkin Gulf Resolution by a vote of 88 to 2. The House of Representatives passed it by a voice vote of 416 to 0.

During the next six months, Vietcong guerrillas attacked several American bases in South Vietnam. They killed Americans in each of these attacks. President Johnson began a rapid buildup of US forces in South Vietnam. They eventually numbered more than half a million in Vietnam.

The Tet Offensive of 1968 brought a turning point in the war. US forces dealt a great military defeat to the Vietcong. But Americans at home had come to oppose the war on both practical and moral terms. President Johnson switched to a policy of winding down the war. He declined to run for reelection, and President Richard M. Nixon succeeded him.

He worked out a cease-fire agreement. US troops withdrew from Vietnam in 1973.

In 1975, the North Vietnamese launched a final offensive. They routed the South Vietnamese army. The war ended in a Communist victory. Vietnam was reunited in 1976 as the Socialist Republic of Vietnam. Some fifty-eight thousand Americans died in the Vietnam War.

A Hi-Tech Modern Army

During the war in Vietnam, the Army tested many new weapons in combat. It introduced helicopters as a means of both troop transport and fire support. Fully developed airmobile tactics emerged. The Army acquired new tanks and armored vehicles. It adopted the M14 and M16 rifles and the M79 grenade launcher. And it re-formed its divisions into three brigades. Not least, it established the Green-Beret-wearing Special Operations Forces.

Soldiers and Marines performed similar duties in Vietnam. But their strategies differed. Both services conducted "search and destroy" ground operations. These operations were designed to find and eliminate the enemy. But after engaging the enemy, Army units would return to their bases and await the next operation.

The Marines favored a combat approach called the "enclave strategy." It called for the occupation and defense of critical terrain and military installations. By holding strategic points, the Marines hoped to free South Vietnamese forces for inland operations. The strategy was meant to keep the South Vietnamese army as a key player in the war. In the end, both strategies failed.

The US Army began the Vietnam War at the peak of training and administrative efficiency. But years of war sapped its manpower and spirit. It became a shell of its earlier combat effectiveness. Discipline and leadership waned. Racial violence and drug abuse grew rampant. Attacks on officers and noncommissioned officers mushroomed in Vietnam and around the globe.

The Army's image and self-esteem suffered deeply from the My Lai Massacre and its attempted cover-up in 1968. In the tiny hamlet of My Lai, US soldiers gunned down unarmed civilians. Public disapproval at home added to the Army's woes. Troop morale plunged. The Army threatened to come apart.

President Nixon ended the draft in 1973. In addition to the Army's other problems, it now faced a new manpower challenge. Only a strong core of dedicated leaders pulled the army back together. The Army reinvented itself in the two decades after the Vietnam War. An all-volunteer army emerged.

In the 1980s, Congress approved large military budgets under President Ronald Reagan. The Army purchased new weapons and equipment. It revamped its training programs to prepare for highly mobilized, fast-moving air-land warfare. This new training was aimed at winning a war against a similarly equipped Soviet army. That clash of superpowers never happened. The collapse of the Soviet Union ended the Soviet threat and the Cold War in December 1991.

Meanwhile, a series of lesser actions served as proving grounds for America's sleek, new, hi-tech modern army. They included Grenada in 1983, Panama in 1988, and later Bosnia/Kosovo in the 1990s. The new army's first big test came in the Middle East.

By the 1990s, the US Army was larger, stronger, tighter, and more modern.

Storm in the Desert

In August 1990, the Iraqi forces of Saddam Hussein invaded the tiny nation of Kuwait. The United States and its UN allies fought against the invaders in the Persian Gulf War. The US-led coalition began a military buildup in the Gulf area. This prewar phase was called Operation Desert Shield. At the same time, diplomatic efforts failed to persuade Saddam Hussein to withdraw his troops from Kuwait.

On December 20, President George H.W. Bush told a reporter that Saddam Hussein needed to understand that "if we get into an armed situation, he's going to get his [rear end]

An American soldier in chemical warfare equipment stands in front of a French armored vehicle in Saudi Arabia during the Gulf War.

A US Army convoy of armored tanks travels across the Saudi Arabian desert during the Gulf War in 1991.

kicked."[9] Saddam did not understand. Bush ordered Saddam to withdraw by January 15, 1991, or face removal by force. Saddam did not comply. Bush ordered an all-out air assault on Iraq and Iraqi troops in Kuwait. It came just one day after his deadline. So began Operation Desert Storm, the shooting phase of the Persian Gulf War.

The air assault lasted six weeks. US Army and Marine forces began a ground attack on March 24, 1991. Seventy-two hours later, Saddam Hussein announced that he would withdraw Iraqi forces from Kuwait. The Persian Gulf War ended. It was a war fought with intensive airpower, armored operations, and advanced military technologies. The US Army was back. But its work in Iraq remained unfinished.

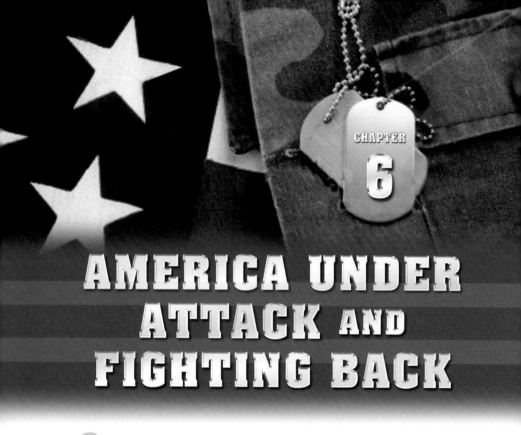

AMERICA UNDER ATTACK AND FIGHTING BACK

On a bright autumn day in New York City, a Boeing 767-200ER of American Airlines Flight 11 smashed into the North Tower of the World Trade Center at 8:46:40 A.M. Minutes later, at 9:11:03 A.M., a second Boeing 767-200ER of United Airlines Flight 175 rammed into the World Trade Center's South Tower. When the second 767 struck, onlookers at the scene and television viewers everywhere knew America was under attack. It was September 11, 2001.

America was under attack! Terrorists had flown planes into the World Trade Center towers and the Pentagon. Almost three thousand Americans died on 9/11. Three days later, US President George W. Bush told the nation:

> *Our responsibility to history is clear: to answer these attacks and rid the world of evil.... This nation is peaceful, but fierce when stirred to anger. The conflict was*

begun on the timing and the terms of others. It will end in a way, and at an hour, of our choosing.[1]

Americans quickly learned that Saudi millionaire Osama bin Laden was behind the 9/11 attacks. His terrorist group Al-Qaeda had carried out his plan. President Bush and Congress moved at once to protect the nation and combat the terrorists.

Securing the Homeland

Bush first established a new Office of Homeland Security. He charged the new agency with many functions and tasks, including improving intelligence and security. Bush wanted to protect Americans on US soil. The US armed forces played a critical part in his plans. Operation Noble Eagle rose up from the still-smoldering ashes of the 9/11 attacks.

Operation Noble Eagle is the name for US military operations in homeland defense. More than thirty-five thousand service personnel have answered the call for help. They include some ten thousand National Guard and Army Reserve troops.[2] National Guard troops helped in the recovery effort in New York City after 9/11. They were among the first on the scene.

Service members also help out in other crises. Their uses include fighting forest fires and controlling civil unrest. When needed, they provide disaster relief for floods and hurricanes. Witness their performance during Hurricanes Katrina and Rita in 2005.

Under Noble Eagle, the Army's main mission has been airport security. Soldiers also guard military bases, dams, and power plants. They further protect tunnels, bridges, rail stations, and emergency command posts.

Urban Search-and-Rescue specialists from the US Army Corps of Engineers participated in response-and-recovery efforts at Ground Zero after terrorist hijackers crashed two airplanes into the Twin Towers of the World Trade Center in New York City.

After taking steps to secure the homeland, President Bush and his team turned their attention to fighting terrorism abroad.

Action in Afghanistan

On September 25, 2001, Secretary of Defense Donald H. Rumsfeld established Operation Enduring Freedom. It was his name for America's war against terrorism. Under this name, the US Army went to war in Afghanistan. It also fights terrorists in other countries.

Afghanistan became the first target of America's war against terror. Al-Qaeda had cells in some sixty countries, but it was based in Afghanistan. Al-Qaeda and the brutal Taliban regime controlled 80 percent of the country. The Northern Alliance held the remaining 20 percent. Afghanistan fell within CentCom's area of responsibility. The area consisted of the Middle East, East Africa, and Central Asia.

Right after 9/11, President Bush met with his top aides. During the conference, General Hugh Shelton, chairman of the Joint Chiefs of Staff, told CentCom commander Tommy Franks, "I need you to come back to us with a plan for Afghanistan."[3]

Franks responded quickly with three options. Option one proposed a simple cruise missile strike. It would target Al-Qaeda training camps and Taliban military bases. The second option added manned bombers—B-1s and B-52s— to option one. Option three specified cruise missiles, manned bombers, and "boots on the ground." CentCom favored option three. For ground operations, it planned to use Special Operations Forces. Other US Army and Marine units would be used as needed. Donald Rumsfeld selected option three. Planning for the operation continued around the clock. Action in Afghanistan was set to begin on October 7, 2001.

A massive air bombardment kicked off the Afghan War. Bombs and missiles took out targets across the face of Afghanistan. Target cities included Herat in the west, Kandahar in the south, Kabul and Jalalabad in the east, and Mazar-e-Sharif in the north. All preselected targets were devastated. Targets of opportunity were smashed next. Boots hit the ground. US Special Operations Forces linked up with Northern Alliance units on October 20.

CentCom's plan called for the Afghans themselves to play a leading role in ousting the Taliban. Tommy Franks wanted the people to help rebuild their government on solid footing. Special Operations Forces were to provide guidance and support.

Special Operations Forces carried custom radios and Global Positioning System (GPS) designators. They could direct close air support and pinpoint air-attack targets. These elite troops would also provide command assistance. Their duties included gathering important information. When needed, they also actively engaged in combat.

Many Special Operations Forces troops rode horses into battle. Afghanistan was riddled with mountains, unpaved roads, and rocky trails. Even Humvees could not navigate the rugged country with the ease of horses. Special Operations Forces soldiers worked in five- to twelve-man teams. They wore winter uniforms that were half American and half Afghan. Bushy beards helped them to blend in with their Afghan comrades of the Northern Alliance. The Afghan War oddly contrasted the old and the new. The ways of

Army soldiers in
Afghanistan set fire to
a Taliban safe house.

In Operation Enduring Freedom in Afghanistan, US Army soldiers fire mortar rounds at suspected Taliban fighting positions in a village in Afghanistan.

ancient warfare merged seamlessly with the latest in modern technology.

On November 7, Alliance fighters began an all-out assault on Mazar-e-Sharif. It was the northern stronghold of Al-Qaeda and the Taliban. Special Forces called in air strikes. The key city fell two days later. A chain reaction followed. All the major Afghan cities surrendered in quick succession. Konduz followed Herat, Kabul, and Jalalabad. The last Taliban bastion at Kandahar fell on December 7.

On December 22, 2001, the Afghans set up an interim government. They placed Hamid Karzai at its head. Osama bin Laden remained at large. Afghans now held the key to their future in their own hands. But CentCom's work had only just begun.

"A Broad and Concerted Campaign"

In late December 2001, President Bush called General Franks to his Texas ranch. Franks informed CentCom deputy commander General Michael De Long, USMC. "We need to pull our current Iraq plan out," he said.[4] Over the next fifteen months, CentCom honed the Iraq plan to a sharp edge.

On Thursday morning, March 20, 2003, Baghdad awakened to the whine of air-raid sirens. It was just after 5:30 A.M. Streetlights still lit the city. Bursts of red and yellow tracer fire streaked the sky, searching for unseen intruders. The crump of bursting antiaircraft shells joined the sirens in a song of destruction. Moments later, cruise missiles and precision bombs rained down on the city. Huge explosions rocked the earth. Smart munitions sought their targets: Iraqi dictator Saddam Hussein and his top aides.

Less than an hour later, President Bush appeared on television. It was 10:15 on Wednesday night in the White House. The president announced the start of the US air attack on Baghdad. He said, "These are the opening stages of what will be a broad and concerted campaign."[5]

Bush then spoke directly to the American armed forces in the Persian Gulf. He said, "The peace of a troubled world and the hopes of an oppressed people now depend on you."[6] In conclusion, Bush promised "to apply decisive force" and vowed "now that the conflict has come . . . we will accept no outcome but victory."[7] Thus, began the first major war of the twenty-first century.

A coalition of armed forces from the United States, Great Britain, Australia, and Poland went to war with Iraq for a second time. The chief causes of the Iraq War were threefold. First, these nations thought Saddam Hussein had weapons of mass destruction. These weapons include nuclear, chemical, and biological weapons. Second, they believed he held ties to terrorists working against the West. And third, they considered Saddam Hussein a ruthless tyrant. As such, he posed a threat to his neighbors and to a region in dire need of stability.

Since 1991, Saddam Hussein had repeatedly defied UN resolutions arising from the Persian Gulf War. The UN hoped to "ensure that Iraq does not pose a threat to international peace and security."[8] But Saddam Hussein chose time and again to defy all sixteen resolutions.

It remains unclear whether these reasons justified going to war with Iraq. Final judgment must await the verdict of time. But the performance of American soldiers and their friends is clear. They carried out their missions with dedication and precision.

On the eve of battle, Captain Anthony Butler, commander of 3rd Battalion HQ, 3rd Infantry Division, spoke to his soldiers. "I don't want you to worry about why we're here," he said. "When we go north, we are the good guys. We are the cavalry."[9]

On March 20, 2003, US and British forces launched a ground assault into Iraq from Kuwait. The next day, US aircraft began an intense bombardment of Baghdad and other targets. The giant air attack was meant to "shock and awe" Iraqi commanders into giving up. Over the next three

M1-Abrams

The modern US Army is the fastest, most powerful war machine in history. It owes much of its speed and mobility to the M1-Abrams main battle tank. The heavily armored M1-Abrams weighs sixty-three tons. It attains a maximum speed of forty-five miles per hour. The Abrams uses almost two gallons of gas to run a mile. Its armament consists of a 120-mm gun, a .50-caliber machine gun, and two .30-caliber machine guns. Its thermal imaging, night vision, laser range finders, and computerized targeting make it the world's most advanced—and most lethal—tank.

weeks, American soldiers and marines dashed 350 miles from Kuwait to downtown Baghdad.

Ten thousand vehicles and seventeen thousand soldiers moved up the Euphrates River. The US Army's 3rd Infantry Division led the western thrust of a twin American offensive. US Marines of the First Marine Expeditionary Force covered the 3rd Division's right flank. The Marines advanced up the Tigris River.

Special Forces seized two key airfields in the west. Soldiers of the 82nd and 101st Airborne Divisions and the 173rd Airborne Brigade fought local battles on the way to the Iraqi capital. Kurdish fighters and Special Forces pressed down from the north. British troops besieged Basra in the south. In less than a month, US-led forces toppled Saddam Hussein's evil regime and ended the major combat.

The fighting spread to Iraq as the US toppled Saddam Hussein's regime. Here, Army soldiers patrol the streets of Tall Kayf, Iraq.

On April 16, 2003, General Tommy Franks met with the press in one of Saddam Hussein's Baghdad palaces. He told reporters that "the decisive combat portion of the campaign is finished."[10] American soldiers had proved the worth of an all-volunteer army. In twenty-one days, the US Army had established itself as the premier army of the twenty-first century.

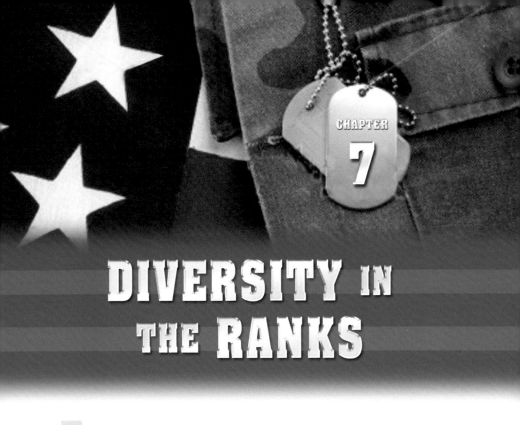

DIVERSITY IN THE RANKS

oday's army recognizes that the diverse characteristics, life experiences, and backgrounds of its soldiers, family members, and civilians enhance its global capabilities and contribute to an adaptive, culturally astute fighting force. It realizes that diversity is key to the development and use of a strategy that contributes to mission readiness. The army seeks to become the national leader in embracing the strengths of a diverse people in an inclusive environment.

Black Heritage in Uniform

African Americans have served with honor in all of America's wars. They fought in state militias during the colonial wars. In the Revolutionary War, they fought at Lexington and Concord. African Americans later served at Bunker Hill, New York, Trenton, Princeton, Savannah, Monmouth, and Yorktown.

After the Revolutionary War, the Army cut its forces. It remained almost all white until the Civil War. On January 1, 1863, President Abraham Lincoln issued the Emancipation Proclamation to free the slaves. It opened enlistments in the Union Army to freedmen. Some 180,000 black soldiers fought for their freedom in 39 major battles and 449 separate actions.[1] Fourteen black soldiers earned the Medal of Honor. Their wartime record helped to earn the vote for black men in the postwar Reconstruction era.

After the Civil War, Congress added four black regiments to the ranks of the regular army. They served primarily in the West. Between 1870 and 1890, fourteen black soldiers earned Medals of Honor. In 1884, Charles Young became the first black man to graduate from West Point. The Army commissioned its first black officer. Black soldiers went on to serve in the Spanish-American War. They later fought in the Philippines and on the Mexican Punitive Expedition of 1916.

World War I came at a time of increased segregation and erosion of rights for African Americans. Lynching of African Americans was all too common. Black leader W.E.B. Du Bois urged African Americans to serve in the military. By serving, he felt, African Americans could regain their rights. Some three hundred eighty thousand black soldiers served in the Army in World War I.[2] Many fought in eight combat regiments.

One French general praised the performance of the African Americans. "The bravery and the dash of your regiments are the admiration of the Moroccan division and they are good judges."[3] Despite their fine service with the French, black soldiers failed to win the Army's confidence.

Native Americans referred to African-American soldiers as "Buffalo Soldiers." Eventually, Congress used the name for all peacetime African-American regiments in the US Army.

After World War I, the Army cut all black infantry regiments. It further excluded blacks from new specialties such as aviation. The Army decided to use black Americans only as laborers in future wars. By 1940, only five thousand black soldiers and five black officers remained in the Army.[4] But when World War II began, the Army again turned to African Americans to fill its ranks.

Nine hundred thousand blacks served in the armed forces in World War II.[5] Both black men and women served mostly in segregated units. Many filled the ranks of motor transport and support units. A handful of black Americans took flight training at the Tuskegee Institute in Alabama. They gained

The achievements of the Tuskegee Airmen, an elite, all-African American group of combat aviators, led to the end of racial segregation and discrimination in the US military.

fame as pilots known as the Black Eagles. One black pilot later said, "We fought two wars: one with the enemy and the other back home in the USA.—Hitler and Jim Crow."[6] ("Jim Crow" symbolizes racial injustice.)

In 1948, President Harry Truman issued Executive Order 9981. His order was aimed at ending segregation in the military. Initially, the Army was slow to act on the order. But combat losses in Korea in 1951 forced the Army to take action. It began mixing black soldiers with all-white units. Black officers still numbered only about 3 percent of the Army's officer corps.

At the peak of the Vietnam War, African Americans represented 11 percent of the US population. But they accounted for 12.6 percent of the American troops in Vietnam. Most blacks served in the infantry. Many of them were draftees. They made up 14.9 percent of US combat casualties.[7] Countless blacks became discontented. Many banded together as "brothers" in a kind of self-imposed segregation.

Black infantryman Haywood T. Kirkland later recalled the pain of Vietnam. He noted: "A lot of brothers who had supply clerk or cook MOS [Military Occupational Specialty] when they came over ended up in the field."[8] What many blacks saw as racial bias fostered their discontent. Some believe that their frustration led to later racial rioting on military bases and naval vessels in 1968. But the armed services acted quickly to curb racism. They set up interracial councils and racial sensitivity training. It was a start.

President Richard Nixon ended the draft in 1973. The Army reinvented itself as an All-Volunteer Force. Black Americans now made up one third of the Army's soldiers. Blacks totaled 10 percent of its officer corps. Four years later, Clifford Alexander became the first black secretary of the Army. In 1989, President George H.W. Bush named General Colin Powell as chairman of the Joint Chiefs of Staff. Powell was the first African American to hold the office.

Powell's policies reduced the size of the military at the end of the Cold War while maintaining US superpower status. He played a central role in the Persian Gulf War in 1991, advocating overwhelming force to achieve quick victory. "Our strategy for dealing with this [Iraqi] army," Powell said, "is very simple: First we're going to cut it off, then we're going to kill it."[9] Powell's vision and exercise of the chairman's

First Among the Finest

Private First Class Milton L. Olive III grew up in a middle-class neighborhood on the south side of Chicago. He left school because he wanted to serve his country. In August 1964, at the age of seventeen, he joined the Army with his father's consent. Fourteen months later, he was serving with the 2nd Battalion, 503rd Infantry of the US Army's 173rd Airborne Brigade in Vietnam. He was a hardened combat veteran at age nineteen.

Milton L. Olive III

On October 22, 1965, Milton Olive and the rest of Company B's 3rd Platoon were pursuing Vietcong (VC) in War Zone D in Vietnam. The thick jungle undergrowth limited their vision. Suddenly, a VC turned and hurled a grenade in the midst of Olive and four of his brothers in arms. Milton saw the grenade first and did not hesitate. Moving quickly away from the others, he fell on the grenade and smothered its blast with his body. "It was the most incredible display of selfless bravery I ever witnessed,"[10] his platoon commander told a journalist later.

The Army awarded PFC Milton L. Olive III the Medal of Honor posthumously for his action at Phu Cuong, Vietnam. He became the first African American to earn the coveted medal in the Vietnam War.

authority helped to shape a modern army for its role in a modern world.

In today's Army, blacks enjoy more equality than ever before. The Army can still improve in racial affairs. But it has made great strides in achieving racial equality. Many civilian institutions would do well to follow its lead. Today's Army also leads the way in gender issues.

Opening Closed Doors

Women's service in the Army dates back to the Revolutionary War. For two centuries, their role was one of support and of freeing men for combat duty. A few women disguised as men fought in the 1700s and 1800s. In World War I, more than twenty-one thousand women served in the Army Nurse Corps.[11] A few more filled clerical positions. But the first large-scale recruitment of women did not take place until World War II. Army chief of staff General George C. Marshall opened the door to women. "I want a women's corps right away and I don't want any excuses,"[12] he declared early in the war.

On May 14, 1942, the Women's Auxiliary Army Corps (WAAC) was formed. Its name was changed to the Women's Army Corps (WAC) on September 1, 1943. Colonel Oveta Culp Hobby served as the first director of the WAAC and WAC. Some one hundred thousand women served in the WAC.[13] The Army continued to use women in support roles to free men for combat. After the war, the role of women in the Army almost disappeared.

In 1948, Congress passed the Women's Armed Services Integration Act. Women became permanent members of the armed services for the first time. At first, the Army restricted women to noncombat specialties. It also limited them to 2 percent of its active-duty personnel. Female officers could not advance beyond the rank of lieutenant colonel. The role of women in the Army broadened in the 1970s. Lagging enlistments and calls for equal treatment drove improvements. The general officer ranks opened up to them.

The status of women in the Army continued to get better in 1973. Improvements came with the end of the draft and the start of the All-Volunteer Force. The Army recruited more women to offset an expected shortfall of male enlistments. Women were allowed to command mixed units of both men and women. Mixed training of male and female recruits began. Benefits for married male and female soldiers were made equal. Pregnant women no longer faced an automatic discharge. Women began pilot training in 1974. The doors to West Point opened to them in 1976.

Women took part in every major troop deployment during the 1990s. They served in Operation Just Cause in Panama. And they participated in Operation Desert Shield and Operation Desert Storm in Iraq. Today, they make up 15 percent of the armed services. In Iraq, one of every seven soldiers is a woman. They serve in all kinds of specialties. Many of them are combat-related. But the Army still prohibits women from serving in the infantry, tanks, and artillery.

Still, the participation of women in the Army draws disapproval by some. Critics complain that their presence may distract males and hinder their performance in combat units. They say that female strength limitations can only weaken combat units. "In every test that's ever been done in Britain as well as the United States and in Israel," says Elaine Donnelly, "it has been found that the physical differences

Since 1948, when women were granted the right to become permanent members of the armed forces, they have increasingly expanded their role in the Army.

really do put women at a disadvantage." Donnelly is an expert on military readiness. She concludes that "it is unwise to have them therefore in land combat units."[14]

Some experts think that women will eventually serve in tanks and artillery. They point out that strength requirements are less demanding than in the infantry. "I think special forces in the infantry are going to be the toughest nuts to crack," predicts Chris Hanson, professor of journalism at the University of Maryland, "and they might never be cracked."[15] But women's progress in the Army over the last half century has been exceptional. One can only wonder how long even the infantry can remain closed to them. For the time

Retired US Army General Ann Elizabeth Dunwoody was the first woman in US military history to achieve a four-star officer rank.

being, the question must remain one of the Army's most controversial issues.

"Don't Ask, Don't Tell" Repealed

One of the most controversial issues facing the armed services today is the status of gay men and women. In the past, all services have discharged gay servicemen and women when their sexual preferences became known. The services discharged one hundred thousand between 1941 and 1996. Discharges averaged about two thousand a year.[16] Those discharged included officers with up to two hundred thousand dollars in training invested in them.

In 1973, gay men and women began to challenge antigay practices in court. The Department of Defense responded sharply. It issued Directive 1332.14 in 1981. The order upheld the discharge of gays. President Bill Clinton tried to overturn the policy in 1993. He wanted to allow gay men and women to serve openly. Gay opponents resisted. Public Law 103-160 achieved a compromise. The compromise was called Don't Ask, Don't Tell (DADT).

The Don't Ask, Don't Tell policy required gay men and women in the military to conceal their sexual orientation. As long as they served in silence, commanders were directed not to investigate their sexuality. After 1994, another ten thousand gay service personnel were discharged.[17] The armed forces continued to grapple with this situation. Meanwhile, gay men and women were still asked to conceal their identities.

On December 15, 2010, the House of Representatives voted to repeal "Don't Ask, Don't Tell" by passing bill H.R. 2965. Three days later, the Senate followed suit by passing bill S. 4023. President Barack Obama signed the repeal into law on December 22, 2010. The end of DADT was set at September 20, 2011.

A Work in Progress

Today's US Army is a work in progress. It is determined to level the playing field for all its soldiers. Work remains to be done. But opportunities for African Americans, other racial minorities, women, and gay men and women to serve are greater than ever before. In return for the service of these men and women, the US Army will work hard to make them all they can be.

ACTIVE AND RESERVE FORCES

The principle role of the US government is to protect and defend the United States of America. Implementation of America's defense falls to the Department of Defense. Thus, the Army, Navy, and Air Force all report to the Secretary of Defense. The Army is made up of two equally important components: active and reserve. Its active component, along with its reserve components—the Army Reserve and the Army National Guard—provide land forces for protecting the American way of life. They serve wherever they are needed around the globe.

Both components of the US Army conduct two kinds of missions. They are called operational and institutional missions. The operational Army consists of numbered armies, corps, divisions, brigades, and battalions. These elements conduct a full range of operations around the world. Unit size depends on need.

The institutional Army supports the operational Army. It provides the resources and facilities for raising, training, equipping, and deploying all Army forces. In short, it ensures the readiness of the operational Army. Every Army unit, installation, or facility reports either to one of the Army Major Commands or to the Headquarters Department of the Army staff.

Army Chain of Command

The Army chain of command begins with the Secretary of the Army, who reports to the Secretary of Defense. The Chief of Staff of the Army reports to the Secretary of the Army and presides over the Department of the Army Headquarters (HQDA) staff. Three Army Commands (ACOM), nine Service Component Commands (ASCC), and eleven Direct Reporting Units (DRU) report to the HQDA staff.

Each Army Command has assigned units and facilities. The Army also supports six geographic Areas of Responsibility (AOR) known as Unified Commands. Three additional Unified Commands support those that are assigned AORs: Special Operations Command (SOCOM), Strategic Command (STRATCOM), and Transportation Command (TRANSCOM).

Organizational Breakdown

In an operational organization, any unit larger than a corps is called an army. Depending upon the scope and size of an operation, an army has three levels—army group, theater army, and field army. The first two armies are formed from the third.

Areas of Responsibility

The US Department of Defense divides the world into six geographic Areas of Responsibility (AOR) known as Unified Commands. These regional commands operate together with other agencies of the US government and regional military partners. Their mutual mission is to promote security and peaceful development in their AORs. These regional Unified Commands are:

◆ Africa Command (AFRICOM)—AOR: African nations not covered by CentCom.

◆ Central Command (CentCom)—AOR: Twenty-five countries in Northeast Africa; Southwest and Central Asia, including much of the Middle East; and the island nation of Seychelles.

◆ European Command (EuCom)—AOR: All of Europe and parts of the Middle East.

◆ Northern Command (NorthCom)—AOR: United States, its territories, and its interests related to homeland defense.

◆ Southern Command (SouthCom)—AOR: Nineteen Central and South American countries (south of Mexico) and twelve Caribbean countries; adjacent waters, including the Gulf of Mexico and part of the Atlantic Ocean.

◆ Pacific Command (PaCom)—AOR: Forty-three countries, twenty territories, and ten US territories; waters from the east coast of Africa to the west coast of the United States, and from the Arctic Ocean to the Antarctic Ocean.

The army group contains two or more field armies. It is the largest ground formation used in combat operations. Its commander is usually a general or lieutenant general.

The theater army is the chief army component in a Unified Command. It takes charge of operations and support. A theater commander directs it.

The field army consists of two to five corps. In turn, a corps contains two to five divisions. A division comprises three brigades, which consists of three or more battalions. Three to five companies make up a battalion. Each company contains three to four platoons made up of three to four squads. A squad, the smallest tactical unit, consists of four to ten soldiers.

The US Army has not deployed an army group since World War II. By comparison, General H. Norman Schwarzkopf commanded a field army in Operation Desert Storm. During Operation Iraqi Freedom, General Tommy Franks used no army unit larger than a corps. Currently, the US Army maintains three field armies—the First, Third, and Fifth.

Fighting Units

Today's Army is a fighting unit sworn to the defense of the United States. It draws on the military skills of five combat branches to fulfill its mission. They are infantry, artillery, armor, aviation, and the corps of engineers.

Infantry soldiers fight on foot with the weapons and ammunition they can carry. Their basic weapons are the rifle and bayonet. They also use grenades, RPGs, machine guns, mortars, and flamethrowers. Handheld antitank weapons lend an added boost in combat. The primary mission of the infantry is to engage, destroy, or capture the enemy.

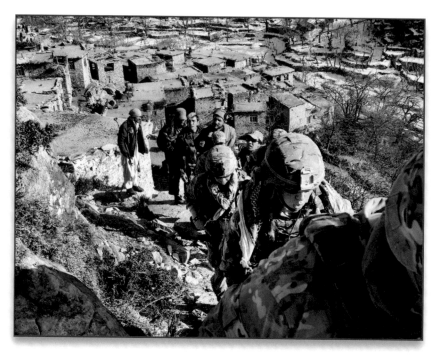

US Army Infantry Soldiers navigate Afghanistan's steep terrain with the Afghan National Army. Infantry soldiers fight on the ground, in the middle of the action.

Artillery dates back to rock-throwing machines in an age before gunpowder. Today's artillery consists of large-caliber gunpowder weapons. They include howitzers, cannons, and rockets. Modern guns use computers to locate targets. Artillery dominates land combat.

Armor became a separate branch of the US Army in 1950. Its main vehicles are the M1-Abrams main battle tank and the Bradley Fighting Vehicle. The cavalry merged with armor. Horses yielded to armored vehicles. These vehicles are supported by infantry, artillery, air power, and helicopters.

Armor uses maneuver, protected firepower, and shock to engage and destroy the enemy.

Army aviation was formed as a separate branch of the US Army in 1983. It consists of those aircraft needed for day-to-day ground operations. Such aircraft are placed under the command and control of a ground commander. Light planes are used for artillery spotting and observation duties. Helicopters serve as troop and cargo transports. They also serve as close fire-support weapons, tank killers, and medical evacuation vehicles.

The corps of engineers was founded in 1775. It constructs roads, bridges, and bases to aid military operations. Engineers build forts and other defenses to protect troops and territory. The corps of engineers also constructs many civil works. Such works include reservoirs, levees, dams, veterans' hospitals, post offices, and more.

Trained and Ready Soldiers

The Army Reserve and the National Guard lend added support to the mission of the US Army. The Army Reserve was created by the National Defense Act of 1916. Its mission is to provide the nation with trained and ready soldiers when needed. Reserve soldiers stand ready to support national strategies at all times.

Today's Army Reserve consists of three levels of service. They are the Selected Reserve, the Individual Ready Reserve, and the Retired Reserve. More than 1 million reservists are standing by to serve the nation when called upon by the president.

The Selected Reserve is the most readily available group of reservists. All Selected Reserve soldiers can be activated

Reserve Officers' Training Corps (ROTC) Cadets prepare to rappel out of a UH-60 Blackhawk Helicopter during the last phase of the Army's Air Assault Course.

in an emergency. Up to thirty thousand Individual Ready Reserve soldiers can also be called up. Many of them have left active duty. But they still have an Army Reserve commitment.

Ready Reserve soldiers number about 651,000 (including Army National Guard). Retired Reserve soldiers total about 383,000. They are retirees from the Active Army, the Army Reserve, and the Army National Guard.[1] Army Reserve soldiers have taken part in every US military operation since 1990.

The Army National Guard is an elite group of citizen-soldiers. Guard members donate a portion of their time to serving their nation. Each state maintains its own National

Guard. In 2015, the Guard celebrated its 379th birthday. Today's National Guard continues its dual mission of serving state and nation. It provides states with units trained and equipped to protect life and property. And it stands ready to defend the United States and its interests around the world.

Turning Civilians into Soldiers

Training is the process by which the US Army turns civilians into soldiers. Reserve and National Guard soldiers generally train one weekend each month. They also take part in a two-week Field Training Exercise once a year. Active-duty enlistees take Basic Combat Training. They then move on to Advanced Individual Training in a military job specialty. Basic Combat Training covers a ten-week schedule:

- **Week 00.** Reception: Indoctrination into Army life.
- **Week 01.** Fall In: Learning Army rules, regulations, and processes in the classroom.
- **Week 02.** Direction: Into the field to test physical and mental endurance; training in first aid and map reading.
- **Week 03.** Endurance: Simulated combat drills challenging mind and body.
- **Week 04.** Marksmanship: Proper techniques of shooting a rifle.
- **Week 05.** Trials: Endurance and marksmanship tests.
- **Week 06.** Camaraderie: Testing platoon bonds and implementing trust exercises.
- **Week 07.** Confidence: Hand grenade training, live fire exercises, foot marching, and confidence testing in the Confidence Course.

- **Week 08.** Victory Forge: A three-day field outing at Victory Forge.
- **Week 09.** Graduation: Inspection, out processing, haircuts, Family Day, and graduation.

After completing Basic Combat Training, new soldiers are ready for the seventeen specialties of Advanced Individual Training (AIT):

- Adjutant General School
- Air Defense Artillery School
- US Army Armor Center
- Aviation Logistics School
- Chemical, Biological, Radiological, Nuclear (CBRN) School
- Department of Defense Fire Academy
- Engineer School
- Field Artillery School
- Financial Management School
- Infantry School
- US Army Intelligence Center
- Military Police School
- Ordnance Mechanical Maintenance School
- Ordnance Munitions and Electronics Maintenance School
- Quartermaster School
- Signal Corps School
- Transportation School

These specialties are defined in greater detail in Army brochures available through Army recruiters and on the Army Web site.

The US Army offers a wide range of training beyond specialty training. Further training includes tactical, technical, physical, and leadership development. Leadership training helps to turn soldiers into leaders. It teaches the skills needed to lead from the front. Unit training in drills and field exercises develops individual and team skills to keep soldiers sharp.

Soldiers seeking to advance their careers even further can seek focused training in specialty schools. Qualified soldiers can receive training in such fields as aviation, medicine, law, information and communications, languages, music, recruiting, and more.

Warrior training offers tough but rewarding challenges. Ranger, Pathfinder, and Special Forces schools test the mettle of the Army's finest soldiers. Rangers excel at leading soldiers on difficult missions. Pathfinders pave the way for airborne soldiers or Army aircraft. Special Forces wage dangerous covert warfare all across the globe.

The broad range of Army training helps to equip soldiers with the confidence and skills needed to take on almost any mission in life.

Army Customs and Practices

Recruits begin to change from their first day in the Army. They start adjusting to new rules. They accept new duties. They develop new outlooks. Recruits embrace the customs and practices that make up the Army way of life. Practices such as military discipline, courtesy, rank, and regulations lend order to their daily routines. The Army way of doing things soon becomes second nature to new soldiers-in-training.

Military discipline is a state of orderly obedience among military personnel. It results from training. Repeated drills, such as gun drill, bayonet drill, and marching, help to instill it. Discipline is essential to an effective military unit. It is the glue that binds soldiers and their actions together.

Courtesy is polite behavior. Most civilian rules of courtesy carry over to Army life. Some courtesies are used only in military services. Officers are addressed as "Sir" out of respect for their ranks. Hand salutes are rendered to officers and the American flag. Military courtesy promotes harmony among individuals from all walks of life.

An old Army saying points out that rank has its privileges. Privileges increase as soldiers advance in rank. In today's Army, soldiers can start at the bottom and climb to the top

A drill sargeant instructs recruits on holding their weapons in formation during Basic Combat Training.

of the career ladder. Rising from private to general is rare but possible.

Motivated soldiers will find that the Army places no limit on advancement and success.

The United States is governed and run by a system of laws, rules, regulations, and procedures. So, too, is the US Army. The Army's system of laws is established by Congress, the Department of Defense, the Department of the Army, and others.

From 1775 to 1950, the Army operated under a set of laws known as the Articles of War. In 1950, Congress enacted a new military justice system. It is called the Uniform Code of Military Justice (UCMJ). The UCMJ applies to all branches of the US military. It continues in effect today with few alterations.

The military justice system is similar to the civilian criminal justice system. But it also deals with various crimes that have no counterpart in civilian law. Mutiny and desertion are good examples. Military law is administered on three levels. They are court-martials, courts of criminal appeals, and the United States Court of Appeals for the Armed Services. The UCMJ is swiftly interpreted, executed, and enforced. By contrast, civilian justice tends to be slow, cumbersome, and less consistent in its decisions.

The UCMJ explains the legal responsibilities of military personnel. It clearly states the legal requirements for protecting and guaranteeing the rights of all service members. It forms the cornerstone of the Army way of life.

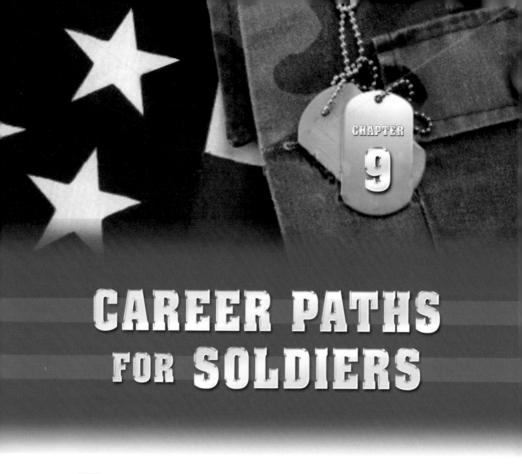

CAREER PATHS FOR SOLDIERS

There is much more to soldiering than putting on a uniform and picking up a rifle. In today's Army, soldiers on active duty serve in more than one hundred and fifty job specialties. The Army Reserve offers some 120 job specialties. Available jobs are classified in ten main groups, or career paths:

◆ **Administrative Support:** Focuses on support jobs in Army personnel, administration, finance, legal, information, and religious services.

◆ **Arts and Media:** Covers the administration, communication, and supervision of Army affairs for both military and civilian audiences. Jobs include broadcast technicians, graphic designers, translators, journalists, and musicians.

◆ **Combat:** Involves aspects of both offensive and defensive combat. Jobs include reconnaissance, security, artillery specialists, special operations, and tank crew. All combat categories are closed to women.

◆ **Computers and Technology:** Technical and informational support for various areas: computers, communications, environmental health, intelligence, explosives, and unmanned vehicle operations.

◆ **Construction and Engineering**: Comprises every facet of construction, including electrical, carpentry, masonry, plumbing, heavy equipment operation, and supervision of construction engineering.

◆ **Intelligence and Combat Support:** Various roles in support of combat operations: intelligence analysts, translators, interpreters, topography specialists, watercraft operators, and food services.

◆ **Legal and Law Enforcement:** Provides services to keep personnel and property safe: military police, criminal investigators, firefighters, security, and emergency specialists.

◆ **Mechanics:** Specialties for maintaining vehicles and machines, ranging from heating and cooling mechanics to vehicle mechanics responsible for servicing aircraft, wheeled and tracked vehicles, heavy equipment, and watercraft.

◆ **Medical and Emergency:** Jobs comprise a variety of specialties in the medical, dental, and veterinary fields, from clinical settings to point of injury.

◆ **Transportation and Aviation:** Tasks focused on coordinating and supervising personnel, equipment, and procedures for proper transportation and use of Army materials around the globe: truck maintainers, railway equipment repairers, air traffic controllers, and parachute riggers.

Career choices are open to those meeting certain general qualifications. Some positions require additional qualifications. Choices begin with enlistment. And enlistments begin with the US Army Recruiter.

A US Army veterinarian tends to a dog in the Philippines during Operation Goodwill. Medical opportunities in the Army are diverse.

The Army Chaplain Corps serves the spiritual needs of soldiers and their families. This important job positively affects the men and women who dedicate their time to their country.

Enlisting

US Army Recruiting Offices are located nationwide. They can be found in telephone directories and online. Army recruiters help applicants decide which service option is best for them. Options include Army Active Duty, Army Reserve, National Guard, Reserve Officers' Training Corps (ROTC), and West Point. Qualification requirements vary with each option.

Musicians can perform in the United States Army Band, which travels all over the world.

Enlisted soldiers are the doers of the Army. They perform specific job skills to ensure the success of a mission. To enlist in the US Army, an applicant must qualify as follows:

◆ Must be at least 17 years old and have not reached the 35th birthday by date of accession.

◆ Written parental consent required for 17-year-olds before processing.

◆ Must pass enlistment physical.

◆ Must meet conduct eligibility requirements/screening.

◆ Must qualify on Armed Services Vocational Aptitude Battery (ASVAB) for enlistment and Military Occupational Specialty (MOS) selected.

Army Reserve and National Guard enlistment requirements are almost the same. Additional requirements apply
for officer candidates:

◆ ROTC applicants must be US citizens who are accepted
or enrolled in a participating college or university.

◆ West Point candidates must be at least seventeen years
old and not have passed 23rd birthday by July 1 of the
year entering the academy; unmarried; a US citizen at
the time of admission; unmarried and must not have a
legal obligation to support a dependent; of good moral
character and able to meet academic, physical and
medical requirements; a high school graduate and submit
Scholastic Assessment Test (SAT) or American College
Testing (ACT) assessment results for evaluation. A
review of scholastic records will be made.

◆ Applicants should obtain a nomination from a member
of Congress or from the Secretary of the Army. Secretary
of the Army nominations are also allowed for enlisted
personnel in the Regular Army, the Army Reserve or the
Army National Guard as well as for ROTC or JROTC
cadets.

Qualified candidates may also earn commissions through
the Army's Warrant Officer Candidate School, Officer
Candidate School, and as a Direct Commission Officer.
Officers are the Army's managers. They possess the skills
and training needed to inspire and encourage others. Officers
provide leadership to enlisted soldiers in all situations.

Army recruiters can provide full details about the different
ways of becoming an officer in today's Army. Recruiters can
also explain the benefits available to both enlisted soldiers
and officers.

Liberal Benefit Package

Army service benefits everyone. It benefits the nation and the service community. Not least, it benefits the soldiers and their families. The Army offers a healthy lifestyle with a sense of purpose. It supports those who serve with a liberal benefit package, including:

◆ Comprehensive healthcare

◆ Subsidized food, housing, and education

◆ Family services and support groups

◆ Special pay for special duties

◆ Cost of living allowances

◆ Generous vacation packages

◆ Pensions for retirement

Compensation Packages

The budget office of Congress recently estimated that the average service member on active duty receives a compensation package valued at $99,000 per year. About 60 percent of the package consists of benefits other than cash. Noncash benefits include healthcare, retirement pay, child care, and free or subsidized food, housing, and education. Active Duty soldiers also earn Basic Pay. Pay is distributed on the first and fifteenth of every month.

Enlisted soldiers may also earn special duty pay, hardship duty pay, foreign language proficiency pay, flight pay, and diving duty and sea pay. Monthly payments range from $75 to $450. Actual amounts depend on the type of duty. The Army also pays reenlistment bonuses. Active-duty soldiers receive up to seventy-two thousand dollars; Reservists, twenty thousand dollars.

The US Army compensates its personnel for their valuable contributions. One benefit is the commisary, a subsidized grocery store that sells food to military families at reduced prices, as compared to civilian markets.

Caring for Soldiers and Their Families

Today's Army provides soldiers and their families with comprehensive health care, life insurance, and generous vacation time. Healthcare comes in the form of an HMO-type plan called TRICARE. It provides medical and dental care at little or no cost. Care is usually provided at a military treatment center. Other programs help soldiers and their families serving at remote sites or overseas. Servicemembers' Group Life Insurance (SGLI) provides soldiers and reservists with a program of low-cost group life insurance.

Soldiers on active duty earn ample vacation time as well as days off. The pressure of military duty demands rest and relaxation for soldiers' well-being.

Time off represents an important part of a soldier's life and well-being. Soldiers on active duty earn thirty days of paid vacation annually. They usually get off on weekends and holidays—except when duty intervenes. The Army also allots sick days to soldiers as needed.

Educational Incentives

The Army encourages soldiers to attend college or take continuing education courses. Soldiers can use the Montgomery GI Bill (MGIB) to pay for a college education. By giving $100 month (total of $1,200) during their first year of service, soldiers may receive more than $61,000 in total benefits to help pay for college. The MGIB will pay a full-time college student $1,717 per month. It pays for up to thirty-six months of education ($61,812 total).[1]

The Army College Loan Repayment Program makes paying off student loans easier. Soldiers enlisting full time for three years may earn up to sixty-five thousand dollars.[2] The Army Reserve and the ROTC offer additional educational incentives.

Additional Services

The Army also offers valuable services, support groups, counseling, and training for the entire family. Many of the services are free or at discount prices. These services include relocation assistance and money management counseling. Family advocacy services offer everything from new parent support to abuse prevention.

The Army offers educational opportunities to its soldiers. They can receive stipends for college, professional schools, and continuing education.

Legal Assistance Centers provide soldiers with advice on personal legal matters. Attorneys on staff review legal documents, such as contracts and leases, and prepare wills, correspondence, and other legal documents. The centers also assist soldiers with free tax preparation and electronic filing.

The Mobilization and Deployment Support program provides pre-deployment and reunion briefings. The program helps soldiers and their families with a variety of family-related topics, such as managing household budgets and maintaining communication with deployed units.

Child and Youth Services offer affordable child-care programs. Costs are adjusted to rank and pay grade. The Army Morale, Welfare, and Recreation Programs deliver a wide array of recreation, sports, entertainment, travel, and leisure activities for soldiers and their families wherever they serve.

Recognizing the importance of families, the Army offers a wide variety of programs for children of soldiers.

Families stationed abroad are taken care of during what could be a difficult transition. Here, military family members are entertained by a visiting guest.

Purpose and Its Price

The Army offers many rewards and benefits to active-duty career soldiers. But potential volunteers should carefully weigh the costs of commitment to an Army career. Time is the first commitment. Both the Regular Army and the Army Reserve require a minimum of two-year enlistments. Enlisted soldiers and officers cannot quit the Army on a whim. They must honor the terms of their enlistment or service contracts.

Some seven hundred thousand soldiers are committed to the defense of the nation. The Army assigns about one quarter of them to direct combat jobs. These jobs involve certain risks, such as physical injury. Psychological trauma like posttraumatic stress disorder (PTSD) can also endanger

Combat Commendations

Bronze Star—Awarded for combat bravery or worthy achievement. A V on the ribbon denotes combat action.

Combat Infantryman Badge—Awarded to soldiers actively engaged in ground combat. It originated in World War II.

Distinguished Service Cross—The medal recognizes bravery in combat that falls short of the Medal of Honor. It is awarded for exceptional heroism at the risk of life.

Medal of Honor—America's highest award for gallantry in combat. It is awarded for combat actions "above and beyond the call of duty."

Purple Heart—The Purple Heart was authorized by George Washington in 1782. It is awarded for wounds received in action against an enemy.

Silver Star—Awarded for gallantry less notable than that needed for a service cross.

mental stability. In the worst case, combat can be life threatening.

Other service hazards arise from overseas deployment and long separations from home and family. Separations can create a variety of personal and financial difficulties.

Army life demands a level of structured living not generally found in civilian life. Those who have a problem with discipline or living by Army rules might do well to opt for other careers. But those with a strong sense of purpose and desire to serve may well find an Army career more than worth the costs of commitment.

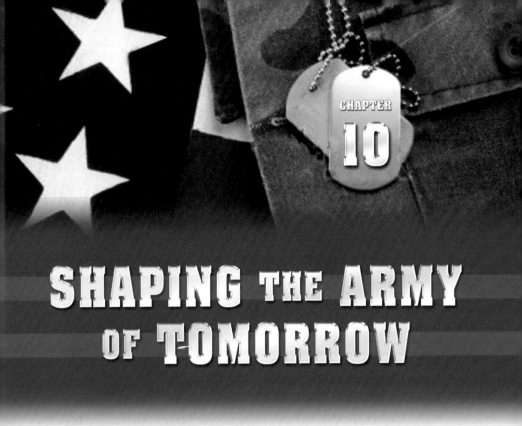

SHAPING THE ARMY OF TOMORROW

oday's Army wants to continue being all it can be. "I think," writes Secretary of the Army John M. McHugh, "both the president and the secretary of defense have made very clear that their main objective, which is ours as well, is to preserve this magnificent land force that's been built over the last 10 years, and ensure we remain in the future what we are today: the greatest land power the world has ever seen."[1]

To maintain the Army's unparalleled excellence, the Secretary of the Army, and Army Chief of Staff General Raymond T. Odierno, recently articulated the Army's vision for the future: "The Army is globally engaged and regionally responsive; it is an indispensable partner and provider of a full range of capabilities to Combatant Commanders in a Joint, Interagency, Intergovernmental, and Multinational (JIIM) environment. As part of the Joint Force and as America's

Army soldiers are proud, well-decorated members of the US military. Here, President Barack Obama awards US Army Staff Sgt. Ty M. Carter the Medal of Honor for conspicuous gallantry.

Army, in all that we offer, we guarantee the agility, versatility and depth to Prevent, Shape and Win.[2]

Soldiers are the cornerstone of the Army vision. Success of the Army's mission centers on their actions and values. They live the life, perform the deeds, and uphold the warrior ethos of the Army. Soldiers represent the nation's best citizens—the best of the best.

From the ranks of the nation's finest citizens, the Army will select and train leaders for this century. Training will yield decisive, adaptive, innovative leaders. Officers will be schooled in the art and science of the profession of arms. They will demonstrate character and integrity at all times. Future leaders will think creatively, pursue lifelong learning, and boldly face challenges and complex problems. They will be all they can be.

On April 3, 2014, in a joint statement presented to the United States Senate Committeee on Armed Services, Secretary McHugh and General Odierno noted:

> *Throughout our history, we have drawn down our armed forces at the close of every war. However, we are currently reducing Army end strength from our wartime high before the longest war in our Nation's history has ended, and in an uncertain international security environment. Our challenge is to reshape into a smaller, yet capable, force in the midst of sustained operational demand for Army forces and reduced budgets.*

The Army participates in humanitarian assistance missions around the globe. At home or abroad, Army personnel represent the best and the brightest.

The Nation faces uncertainty and, in the face of such uncertainty, needs a strong Army that is trained, equipped and ready. . . . Despite our best efforts, there remains a high likelihood that the United states will once again find itself at war sometime during the next two decades. It is our job to be prepared for it.[3]

"Our Army's . . . history is punctuated by episodic shifts in the global security environment that have called for organizational change, " notes General Odierno. "I firmly believe we are experiencing one of those shifts now, given the end of the Iraq war, transition plans in Afghanistan, and opportunities to enhance stability worldwide by engaging our allies and partners."[4]

Lastly, General Odierno writes

[T]he Army's role is to prevent, shape, and win. We will prevent conflict by maintaining credibility based on capacity, readiness and modernization; we will shape the environment by sustaining strong relationships with other Armies; and, if prevention fails, we will rapidly apply the Army's combined arms capabilities to dominate and win decisively. . . . The vision statement is a succinct expression of our future. It reflects both our values and our purpose, and should guide us as we shape the Army of tomorrow.[5]

APPENDIX: SALARIES IN THE ARMY

Ranks and Salaries of Enlisted Men

Enlisted Rank	Pay Grade	Approximate Salary*	Insignia
Private	E-1	under 4 months: $1,430 per month; over 4 months: $1546.80 per month	No insignia
Private E-2	E-2	$1,734.00 per month	
Private First Class	E-3**	$1,823.40–2,055.30 per month	
Specialist	E-4	$2,019.60–2,451.60 per month	
Corporal	E-4	$2,019.60–2,451.60 per month	
Sergeant	E-5	$2,202.90–3,125.70 per month	
Staff Sergeant	E-6	$2,404.50–3,724.20 per month	
Sergeant First Class	E-7	$2,780.10–4,996.20 per month	
Master Sergeant	E-8	$3,999.00–5,703.60 per month	
First Sergeant	E-8	$3,999.00–5,703.60 per month	
Sergeant Major	E-9	$4,885.20–7,584.60 per month	
Command Sergeant Major	E-9	$4,885.20–7,584.60 per month	
Sergeant Major of the Army	E-9	$4,885.20–7,584.60 per month	

* Approximate salaries are as of 2015 and do not include food and housing allowances, free healthcare, money for college, and bonuses.

** Salary for ranks E-3 through E-9 depend on the number of years in service.

Ranks and Salaries of Officers

Warrant Officers Rank	Pay Grade	Approximate Salary per month*	Insignia
Warrant Officer	W-1	$2,868.30–4,956.00	No insignia
Chief Warrant Officer	W-2	$3,267.30–5,453.70	
Chief Warrant Officer	W-3	$3,692.40–6,477.30	
Chief Warrant Officer	W-4	$4,043.40–7,531.80	
Chief Warrant Officer	W-5	$7,189.50–9,408.30	
Officers			
Second Lieutenant	O-1	$2,934.30–3,692.10	
First Lieutenant	O-2	$3,380.70–4,678.50	
Captain	O-3	$3,912.60–6,365.40	
Major	O-4	$4,449.90–7,430.10	
Lieutenant Colonel	O-5	$5,157.60–8,762.40	
Colonel	O-6	$6,186.60–10,952.40	
Brigadier General	O-7	$8,264.40–12,347.70	
Major General	O-8	$9,946.20–14,338.50	
Lieutenant General	O-9	$14,056.80–17,436.90	
General	O-10	$16,072.20–19,762.50	
General of the Army	Special	Special	

* Salaries are as of 2015 and do not include food and housing allowances, free healthcare, money for college, and bonuses; also, an approximate salary range has been given for each rank.

TIMELINE

1690–1775—Era of colonial/state militias.

1775—Continental Army founded on June 14.

1775–1783—American Revolutionary War.

1802—US Military Academy founded at West Point, New York.

1812–1814—War of 1812.

1846–1848—Mexican-American War.

1850–1890—Indian Wars.

1861–1865—American Civil War.

1863—The North adopts the draft.

1898—Spanish-American War.

1899–1902—Philippine Insurrection.

1916—National Defense Act expands regular forces and the National Guard and lays foundation for the Reserve Officer Training Corps (ROTC).

1917—Selective Service Act of 1917 establishes draft.

1917–1918—American Expeditionary Force fights in Europe in World War I.

1920—National Defense Act enlarges Army general staff and returns Army to a volunteer force.

1939–1945—World War II.

1940—Congress adopts first prewar conscription act.

1941—Japanese planes bomb Pearl Harbor on December 7; America enters World War II.

1942—Women's Auxiliary Army Corps (WAAC) established.

1943—Women's Auxiliary Army Corps becomes Women's Army Corps (WAC).

1944—GI Bill commences under the Servicemen's Readjustment Act.

1947—The Army becomes part of the Department of Defense under the National Defense Act of 1947 (and under subsequent acts of 1949 and 1958).

1948—President Truman issues Executive Order 9981 ordering an end to segregation in the military; Congress adopts new draft law; passes Women's Armed Services Integration Act, providing a permanent role for women in the military.

1950–1953—Korean War.

1952—Army Special Forces (Green Berets) organized.

1961–1975—Vietnam War.

1973—All-Volunteer Force established in the military.

1975—Compulsory draft registration ends.

1976—Women enter the US Military Academy at West Point.

1991—Persian Gulf War.

2001—Terrorists attack World Trade Center Towers and the Pentagon on September 11; Operation Noble Eagle begins; Operation Enduring Freedom commences in Afghanistan on October 7.

2003—Operation Iraqi Freedom begins on March 20.

2004—Four private contractors working for Blackwater USA are killed in an ambush in Fallujah.

2005—President George W. Bush says the United States went to war based on faulty intelligence.

2006—Saddam Hussein is hanged.

2007— President George W. Bush announces plans for a troop surge involving 20,000 soldiers and marines.

2010—The last American combat brigade leaves Iraq, marking an end to combat operations.

2010—Osama bin Laden is killed in Abbottabad, Pakistan, by members of Navy SEAL Team 6.

2011—The last US troops leave Iraq.

Timeline

2012—Hundreds of Afghans hold violent protests against the alleged burning of Qurans at the Bagram Airbase north of Kabul.

2013—Soldiers continue to train Afghan police and security forces as US forces continue to draw down.

2014—Withdrawal continues and the insurgency increases.

2015—The United States stands by plans to halve the number of its troops in Afghanistan this year and reduce them further in 2016.

CHAPTER NOTES

CHAPTER 1   Soldier Stories

1. Todd S. Purdum and the Staff of *The New York Times, A Time of Our Choosing: America's War in Iraq* (New York: Times Books, 2003), p. 135.
2. Michael DeLong, with Noah Lukeman, *Inside CentCom: The Unvarnished Truth About the Wars in Afghanistan and Iraq* (Washington, D.C.: Regnery Publishing, 2004), p. 108.
3. Ibid., p. 110.
4. Martin Walker, ed., *The Iraq War: As Witnessed by the Correspondents and Photographers of United Press International* (Washington, D.C.: Brassey's, 2004), p. 126.
5. Ibid.
6. Scott Stump, "Jessica Lynch: Iraq still haunts my dreams 10 years after rescue," TODAY online, April 1, 2013, <http://www.today.com/news/jessica-lynch-iraq-still-haunts-my-dreams-10-years-after-1C9160653> (January 28, 2015).
7. "Mission," *The Official Homepage of the United States Army*, n.d., <http://www.army.mil/organization/> (January 25, 2015).
8. "Warrior Ethos," *The Official Homepage of the United States Army*, n.d., < <http://www.army.mil/values/warrior.html/> (January 25, 2015).

CHAPTER 2   Evolution of an American Army

1. Robert Leckie, *The Wars of America*, New and Updated ed. (New York: HarperCollins Publishers, 1993), p. 106.
2. Douglas Brinkley, *American Heritage History of the United States* (New York: Viking, 1998), pp. 80–81.
3. Ibid., p. 80.
4. Max R. Williams, "American Revolutionary War," in *Brassey's Encyclopedia of Military History and Biography*, ed. Franklin D. Margiotta (Washington, D.C.: Brassey's, 1994), p. 51.
5. Leckie, p. 224.

6. William B. Skelton, "Army, US: 1783–1865," in *The Oxford Companion to American Military History*, ed. John Whiteclay Chambers II (New York: Oxford University Press, 1999), p. 50.

7. Ibid.

8. R. Ernest Dupuy and Trevor N. Dupuy, *The Harper Encyclopedia of Military History, From 3500 B.C. to the Present*, Fourth ed. (New York: HarperCollins, 1993), p. 882.

9. Maurice Matloff, ed., *American Military History* (Conshohocken, Penn.: Combined Books, 1996), p. 178.

CHAPTER 3   War and Westward Ho!

1. R. Ernest Dupuy and Trevor N. Dupuy, *The Harper Encyclopedia of Military History, From 3500 B.C. to the Present*, Fourth ed. (New York: HarperCollins, 1993), p. 950.

2. Bruce Catton, *The Civil War*, The American Heritage Library (New York: American Heritage, 1985), p. 23.

3. Dupuy and Dupuy, p. 951.

4. Maurice Matloff, ed., *American Military History* (Conshohocken, Penn.: Combined Books, 1996), p. 189.

5. Gerald S. Henig and Eric Niderost, *Civil War Firsts: The Legacies of America's Bloodiest Conflict* (Mechanicsburg, Penn.: Stackpole Books, 2001), p. 38.

6. Ibid.

7. James Marshall-Cornwall, *Grant as Military Commander* (New York: Barnes & Noble Books, 1995), p. 61.

8. David Eggenberger, *An Encyclopedia of Battles—Accounts of Over 1,560 Battles from 1479 B.C. to the Present* (New York: Dover Publications, 1985), p. 65.

9. Joseph G. Dawson III, "Army, US: 1866–99," in *The Oxford Companion to American Military History*, ed. John Whiteclay Chambers II (New York: Oxford University Press, 1999), p. 51.

10. Clinton, Catherine, *Scholastic Encyclopedia of the Civil War*. (New York: Scholastic, 1999), p. 28.

11. Douglas Brinkley, *American Heritage History of the United States* (New York: Viking, 1998), p. 239.

12. Robert M. Utley, "Little Bighorn, Battle of the," in The *Oxford Companion to American Military History*, ed. John Whiteclay Chambers II (New York: Oxford University Press, 1999), p. 397.

13. John Mack Faragher, *The American Heritage Encyclopedia of American History* (New York: Henry Holt and Company, 1998), p. 532.

14. Richard N. Ellis, "Army on the Frontier," in *The New Encyclopedia of the American West*, ed. Howard R. Lamar (New Haven, Conn.: Yale University Press, 1998), p. 54.

15. Graham A. Cosmas, "Spanish-American War (1898–99)," in *The American Heritage Encyclopedia of American History*, p. 876.

CHAPTER 4 World at War

1. Douglas Brinkley, *American Heritage History of the United States* (New York: Viking, 1998), p. 343.

2. Ibid., p. 348.

3. James L. Abrahamson, "Army, US: 1900–41," in The *Oxford Companion to American Military History*, ed. John Whiteclay Chambers II (New York: Oxford University Press, 1999), p. 52.

4. James H. Hallas, ed., *Doughboy War: The American Expeditionary Force in World War I* (Boulder, Colo.: Lynne Rienner Publishers, 2000), p. 310.

5. Adolf Hitler, *Mein Kampf*, trans. Ralph Manheim (Boston: Houghton Mifflin, 1971), p. 632.

6. Maurice Matloff, ed., *American Military History* (Conshohocken, Penn.: Combined Books, 1996), p. 64.

7. Douglas Brinkley, ed., *World War II: The Axis Assault, 1939–1942. The New York Times Living History* (New York: Times Books/Henry Holt, 2003), p. 185.

8. Ibid., p. 187.

9. C. L. Sulzberger, *World War II*, The American Heritage Library (New York: American Heritage, 1985), p. 75.

10. Ibid., p. 183.

Chapter Notes

CHAPTER 5   Cold Relations and Hot Wars

1. Maurice Matloff, ed., *American Military History* (Conshohocken, Penn.: Combined Books, 1996), p. 201.
2. Graham A. Cosmas, "Army, US: Since 1941," in *The Oxford Companion to American Military History*, ed. John Whiteclay Chambers II (New York: Oxford University Press, 1999), p. 53.
3. Robert Leckie, *Conflict: The History of the Korean War, 1950–1953* (New York: Da Capo Press, 1996), p. 53.
4. Ibid., p. 95.
5. John Mack Faragher, *The American Heritage Encyclopedia of American History* (New York: Henry Holt and Company, 1998), p. 969.
6. Ibid.
7. Ibid.
8. Harry G. Summers, Jr., *Vietnam War Almanac* (New York: Facts On File, 1985), p. 342.
9. Roger Hilsman, *George Bush vs. Saddam Hussein: Military Success! Political Failure?* (Novato, Calif.: Lyford Books, 1992), p. 92.

CHAPTER 6   America Under Attack and Fighting Back

1. Michael DeLong, with Noah Lukeman, *Inside CentCom: The Unvarnished Truth About the Wars in Afghanistan and Iraq* (Washington, D.C.: Regnery Publishing, 2004), p. 17.
2. "Operation Noble Eagle," *GlobalSecurity.org*, n.d., <http://www.globalsecurity.org/military/ops/noble-eagle.htm> (January 25, 2015).
3. DeLong and Lukeman, p. 22.
4. Ibid., p. 63.
5. Todd S. Purdum and the Staff of *The New York Times, A Time of Our Choosing: America's War in Iraq* (New York: Times Books, 2003), p. 111.
6. Ibid.
7. Ibid.

8. "Saddam Hussein's Defiance of United Nations Resolutions," *The White House*, n.d., <http://georgewbush-whitehouse. archives.gov/infocus/iraq/decade/sect2.html> (January 25, 2015).

9. Editors of Time, *21 Days to Baghdad: The Inside Story of How America Won the War Against Iraq* (New York: Time Books, 2003), p. 20.

10. Dan Rather and the Reporters of CBS News, *America at War, The Battle for Iraq: A View From the Frontlines* (New York: Simon & Schuster, 2003), p. 7.

CHAPTER 7   Diversity in the Ranks

1. Gerald S. Henig and Eric Niderost, *Civil War Firsts: The Legacies of America's Bloodiest Conflict* (Mechanicsburg, Penn.: Stackpole Books, 2001), p. 48.

2. John Sibley Butler, "African Americans in the Military," in *The Oxford Companion to American Military History*, ed. John Whiteclay Chambers II (New York: Oxford University Press, 1999), p. 8.

3. Edward M. Coffman, *The War to End All Wars* (Madison: University of Wisconsin Press, 1986), p. 233.

4. Butler, p. 8.

5. Ibid.

6. Norman Polmar and Thomas B. Allen, *World War II: The Encyclopedia of the War Years, 1941–1945* (New York: Random House, 1996), p. 157.

7. Butler, p. 9

8. Peter S. Kindsvatter, *American Soldiers: Ground Combat in the World Wars, Korea, and Vietnam* (Lawrence: University Press of Kansas, 2003), p. 280.

9. Majid Khadduri and Edmund Ghareeb, *War in the Gulf, 1990–91: The Iraq-Kuwait Conflict and Its Implications* (New York: Oxford University Press, 1997), p. 172.

10. Bethanne Kelly Patrick, "Pfc. Milton Lee Olive III." Military.com., <http://www.military.com/Content/MoreContent?file=ML_olive_bkp> (January 25, 2015).

11. Constance J. Moore and Jan Herman, "Nurse Corps, Army and Navy," in *The Oxford Companion to American Military History*, ed. John Whiteclay Chambers II (New York: Oxford University Press, 1999), p. 514.

12. Polmar and Allen, p. 869.

13. Bettie J. Morden, "WAC," in *The Oxford Companion to American Military History*, ed. John Whiteclay Chambers II (New York: Oxford University Press, 1999), p. 772.

14. Zlatica Hoke, "US Military Women Closer Than Ever to Combat Zone," *Voice of America News*, October 31, 2009, < http://www.voanews.com/content/a-13-2004-12-01-voa85/397621.html> (January 25, 2015).

15. Ibid.

16. Aaron Belkin, "Gay Men and Lesbians in the Military," in *The Oxford Companion to American Military History*, ed. John Whiteclay Chambers II (New York: Oxford University Press, 1999), p. 287.

17. "Report: 'Don't Ask, Don't Tell' costs $363M," *USATODAY.com*, February 14, 2006, < http://usatoday30.usatoday.com/news/washington/2006-02-14-dont-ask-report_x.htm> (January 25, 2015).

CHAPTER 8   Active and Reserve Forces

1. "National Security and Veterans Affairs," United States Census Bureau, n.d., <http://www.census.gov/prod/2011pubs/12statab/defense.pdf> (January 25, 2015).

CHAPTER 9   Career Paths for Soldiers

1. "Montgomery GI Bill Rates," Military.com., <http:www.military.com/education/gi-bill/active-duty-gi-bill-payment-rates.html> (January 27, 2015).

2. "The Army Student Loan Repayment Program," Forget Student Loan Debt, <http://www.forgetstudentloandebt.com/student-loan-relief-programs/federal-student-loan-relief/federal-forgiveness-programs/military-programs/army-loan-repayment-program/> (January 27, 2015).

CHAPTER 10   Shaping the Army of Tomorrow

1. John McHugh, "Secretary of the Army John McHugh," *Soldiers Magazine*. June 2012. <http://www.army.mil/leaders/sa> (January 2015).

2. General Ray Odierno, "The Army's Vision," <http://armylive.dodlive.mil/index.php/2012/05/army-vision/> (January 2015).

3. Secretary of the Army John M. McHugh and Chief of Staff of the Army General Raymond T. Odierno, "On the Posture of The United States Army," United States Senate Committeee on the Armed Services, April 3, 2014. <http://www.armed-services.senate.gov/imo/media/doc/McHugh-Odierno_04-03-14.pdf> (January 28, 2015).

4. Odierno, "The Army's Vision."

5. Ibid.

GLOSSARY

AEF—American Expeditionary Force.

AK-47—Kalashnikov selective-fire, gas-operated 7.62 x 39 mm assault rifle.

Blackhawk—UH-60 four-bladed, twin-engine, medium-lift utility helicopter.

Bradley—M2 infantry fighting vehicle or M3 cavalry fighting vehicle.

buffalo soldiers—American Indian name for African-American soldiers serving in the western United States after the Civil War.

CentCom—Central Command; one of several US Unified/Joint Commands; oversees operations in Iraq.

ethos—Guiding beliefs of a person, group, or institution.

fedayeen—Paramilitary units of Saddam Hussein's secret police; guerrilla insurgents, generally dressed in civilian clothes and wearing black masks.

GI—American soldier; name derives from "government issue."

Hessians—Eighteenth-century German auxiliaries contracted for military service by the British government.

Humvee—High-mobility, multipurpose wheeled vehicle (HMMWV or Hummer).

Lend Lease—Program under which the United States supplied Free France, Great Britain, the Republic of China, and later the USSR and other Allied nations with food, oil, and materiel between 1941 and August 1945.

M1-Abrams—Main US battle tank.

M16—US 5.56 mm semiautomatic rifle.

M16A2—Standard US 5.56-mm infantry rifle; gas-operated, it can fire single shots or three-round bursts. (A variant of the M16A2 rifle is the M16A4).

militia—A civil military force that supplements a regular army in an emergency.

minutemen—During the American Revolution, militia members able to assemble under arms at a minute's notice.

Patriot—US MIM-104 mobile long range surface-to-air missile with antiballistic missile capability.

Reconstruction—Generally refers to the period in US history immediately following the Civil War in which the federal government set the conditions that would allow the rebellious Southern states back into the Union.

RPG—Rocket-propelled grenade.

SEAL—Sea-air-land commando of the US Navy.

Tonkin Gulf Resolution—A joint resolution passed by the US Congress in response to the Gulf of Tonkin incident, giving US President Lyndon B. Johnson authorization for the use of "conventional" military force in Southeast Asia.

Wehrmacht—German armed forces.

FURTHER READING

Books

Burgan, Michael. *World War II Pilots: An Interactive History Adventure (You Choose: World War II)*. North Mankato, Minn.: Capstone Press, 2013.

Cooke, Tim. *US Army Special Forces*. Ultimate Special Forces series. New York: Rosen Publishing, 2013.

———. *US Army Rangers*. Ultimate Special Forces series. New York: Rosen Publishing, 2013.

Knapp, Ron. *U.S. Generals of World War II*. Inspiring Collective Biographies series. Berkeley Heights, N.J.: Enslow Publishers, 2013.

Otfinoski, Steven. *World War II Infantrymen. An Interactive History Adventure (You Choose: World War II)*. North Mankato, Minn.: Capstone Press, 2013.

Stein, R. Conrad. *World War II in Europe: From Normandy to Berlin*. The United States at War series. Berkeley Heights, N.J.: Enslow Publishers, 2011.

Swain, Gwenyth. *World War I: An Interactive History Adventure (You Choose: History)*. North Mankato, Minn.: Capstone Press, 2012.

Web Sites

goarmy.com
An informative recruiting site for the US Army.

army.mil/
The official US Army Web site.

goarmy.com/reserve.html
The US Army Reserve's official site.

Movies

The Hurt Locker. **Directed by Kathryn Bigelow. Burbank, Calif.: Warner Brothers, 2008.**
This movie follows an Explosive Ordnance Disposal (EOD) army unit in the Iraq War.

Saving Private Ryan. **Directed by Steven Spielberg. Universal City, Calif.: Dreamworks Studios, 1998.**

INDEX

A

Adams, John, 17
Advanced Individual Training
   (AIT), 87–88
African Americans, 27, 28, 69–75
Africa Command (AfriCom), 125
All-Volunteer Force, 37–38, 54,
   68, 73, 76
Al-Qaeda, 59, 61, 64
Ambush Alley, 6, 10
American Expeditionary Force
   (AEF), 33, 35, 37, 39
American Revolution, 14–16,
   69–70, 75
armor, 38, 53, 57, 67, 83–85
Army, US
   benefits of service, 76, 97–104
   career paths in, 92–94
   civil role of, 27–28, 59, 69, 75,
   85, 90, 92
   compensation packages, 98
   corps of engineers, 17–18, 83,
   85
   educational benefits in,
   100–101
   enlistment eligibility,
   94–97
   establishment of, 16
   mission of, 12
   morale of, 54, 102
   organization of, 81–87
   training, 85–91
   vision of, 105–108
Army of the Constitution, 16

artillery, 17, 32–33, 76–77, 83–85,
   88, 93
atomic bomb, 44, 46
aviation, 71, 83, 85, 88–89, 93–94

B

Baghdad, 5, 12, 65–68
Basic Combat Training, 87–89
bin Laden, Osama, 59, 65
Blackhawk helicopter, 9
Bradley Fighting Vehicle, 84–85
Bush, George H.W., 56–57, 73
Bush, George W., 58–59, 61–62,
   65–66

C

Canada, 17, 46
cavalry, 16–17, 26, 28, 30, 38, 66,
   84
Central Command (CentCom),
   7–8, 61–62, 65, 82
Civil War, 21–28, 33, 70
Cold War, 45, 54, 73
combat jobs, 93, 103
commandos, 9–10
Continental Army, 14–16
convoys, 5–7
Custer, George Armstrong, 28

D

Davis, Jefferson, 22
Desert Shield, Operation, 56–57,
   76–78
Desert Storm, Operation, 57, 76,
   83
divisions, US Army

first peacetime, 33
organization of, 80, 83
size of, 39–40, 46
draft, 22, 33, 38, 54

E

Eisenhower, Dwight D., 40, 50
Enduring Freedom, Operation, 61–62, 64
European Command (EuCom), 82

F

family services, 98–105
field armies, 83
France, 17, 32, 34, 35, 38, 40, 42, 45–46
Franks, Tommy R., 7–8, 61–62, 65, 68, 83
French and Indian War, 13

G

Gage, Thomas, 13
Gatling guns, 28–29
gay, men and women, 78–79
George III, 13
Germany, 32–33, 35, 37–40
Grant, Ulysses S., 19–20, 23, 25
Great Britain, 13, 17–18, 32–33, 35, 38–39, 45, 66, 76
Green Berets, 50, 53

H

heroes. *See* soldiers.
Hessians, 16
Hitler, Adolph, 37–39, 72
Hobby, Oveta Culp, 75
Homeland Security, Office of, 59, 61

howitzers, 16, 26, 29, 38, 84
Humvees, 8, 62
Hussein, Saddam, 56–57, 65–68

I

infantry
    African-American, 71, 73–74
    overview, 83
    size of, 38, 80–81
    women and, 76–78
Iraqi Freedom, Operation, 5–10, 83

J

Japan, 39–40, 44, 46
Jefferson, Thomas, 17
Johnson, Lyndon B., 50, 52
Joint Chiefs of Staff, 61, 73

K

Karzai, Hamid, 65
Kennedy, John F., 50
Khrushchev, Nikita, 50
Korean War, 46–49, 72

L

law enforcement, role of Army, 93
Lee, Robert E., 19–20, 24–25
Lend Lease, 39
Lincoln, Abraham, 21–22, 25, 70
Little Big Horn, Battle of, 28
Lynch, Jessica, 7–10

M

MacArthur, Douglas, 40, 44, 46–48
machine guns, 32–33, 49, 67, 83
Madison, James, 18

Marines, US, 9, 47, 53, 57, 61–62, 67
Marshall, George C., 75–76
McHugh, John M., 105, 107
McKinley, William, 30
Medal of Honor, 36, 42, 49, 70, 74, 104
Mexican War, 19–21
militias, colonial, 13–16
Minh, Ho Chi, 50
minorities, 69–79
minutemen, 14
Monroe, James, 18
Montgomery GI Bill (MGIB), 100–101

N

Nasiriyah, Iraq, ambush, 5–10
National Guard, 33, 37–38, 59, 80, 85–87, 95, 97
Native Americans, 16, 19, 21, 27–30, 49
Nixon, Richard M., 52, 54, 73
Noble Eagle, Operation, 59, 61
North Atlantic Treaty Organization (NATO), 45–46
Northern Command (NorthCom), 82
North Korea, 46–48
nuclear weapons, 50, 66

O

Obama, Barack, 79
Odierno, Raymond T., 105–108
officers, commissions, 97

P

Pacific Command (PaCom), 82
Pacific, World War II in, 39–40, 44

Panama invasion, 54, 76
Pathfinders, 89
Patriot missile system, 5
Pershing, John J., 33, 35, 37
Persian Gulf War, 56–57, 65–66, 73, 75
Powell, Colin, 73, 75

R

Rangers, Army, 9–10, 89.
Ready Reserve, 85–86
Reagan, Ronald, 54
Reconstruction, post-Civil War, 27, 70
Red Cloud, Mitchell, 49
regulations, 18, 87, 87, 91
rescue missions, 7–10
Reserve Officer Training Corps (ROTC), 33, 95, 97, 101
Reserves, Army, 38, 59, 80, 85–87, 92, 95, 97, 101, 103, 105
Retired Reserve, 85–86
rifles, 16, 25–26, 28, 33, 36, 38, 49, 53, 83, 87, 92
rocket-propelled grenades (RPGs), 6, 83
Rommel, Erwin, 40
Roosevelt, Franklin D., 38–39
rules, 18, 87, 89–91, 104
Rumsfeld, Donald H., 61–62
Russia, 32, 35. *See also* Soviet Union.

S

Schwarzkopf, H. Norman, 83
Scott, Winfield, 17, 19–20
Secretary of the Army, 73, 81, 97, 105
Secretary of Defense, 61, 80, 81, 105

segregation, racial, 70–73
Selected Reserve, 85–86
September 11 terrorist attacks, 58–59, 61
soldiers
African American, 27–28, 69–75
captured, 7–10
heroes, 36, 42, 104
principles of, 12
role of, 50, 80
women, 10, 71, 75–78, 79, 93
Southern Command (SouthCom), 82
Soviet Union, 39, 45–46, 50, 54
Spanish-American War, 30–31
Special Forces, 9–10, 50–51, 64–65, 67, 77, 89
Special Operations Command (SOCOM), 81
Special Operation Forces, 53, 61–64, 93
Strategic Command (STRATCOM), 81

T

Taliban, 61–62, 64
tanks, 8, 32, 38, 42, 53, 67, 76–77, 83–85, 93
Taylor, Zachary, 19
Tonkin Gulf, 50, 52
Tonkin Gulf Resolution, 52–53
Transportation Command (TRANSCOM), 81
Truman, Harry S., 46, 72

U

Uniform Code of Military Justice (UCMJ), 91
uniforms, 15, 62, 92
United Nations (UN), 45–48, 56, 66
US Military Academy at West Point, 17–18, 70, 76, 95, 97

V

Vietnam War, 50, 52–54, 72–74

W

War of 1812, 17
Warrior Ethos, 12, 106
War on Terrorism, 58–59, 61–62, 64
Washington, George, 14–17, 104
Wilson, Woodrow, 33
women, in the Army, 10, 71, 75–79, 93
Women's Army Corps (WAC), 75
World War I, 32–33, 35–37, 48, 70–71, 75
World War II, 8, 38–40, 42, 44, 45–46, 48, 71–72, 75, 83, 104